How to LIVE, LEAD, *and* WORK
with INTENTION

Take It
All Apart

LINDSAY LEAHY

RIVER GROVE
BOOKS

Published by River Grove Books
Austin, TX
www.rivergrovebooks.com

Distributed by River Grove Books

Design and composition by Greenleaf Book Group and Mimi Bark
Cover design by Greenleaf Book Group and Mimi Bark
Cover image used under license from ©Shutterstock.com/Vector FX

Publisher's Cataloging-in-Publication data is available.

Print ISBN: 978-1-63299-870-5

eBook ISBN: 978-1-63299-871-2

First Edition

To Mitch, my incredible husband:
Thank you for always believing in me, challenging me,
and loving me in a way that only you ever could through all of
the transitions and changes and multiple versions of me.
You are my person.

I hope this book blesses
your journey!
What you do matters, & who
you become matters more.

Dream Big.
Love Hard.
Shine On.

♥ Lindsay

Contents

Introduction

The top regret of the dying is wishing they'd lived a life true to themselves, not the life others expected of them. The first time I read this, it stopped me in my tracks because I realized I was actively walking down this same path of regret. A life true to myself? I didn't have a clue what that looked like or meant.

What I did know is that I was overwhelmed, exhausted, and frustrated by my life, despite it being a good one. Something was missing. I wasn't sure how to move forward, but I knew something needed to change.

Have you ever felt that way? Maybe you do right now. Stuck, anxious, held back by past experiences, shackled by emotions, or the expectations of others? So focused on others you aren't sure what you want or need? Maybe you're seeking deeper connections or relationships that are more satisfying, or you simply want to continue your growth and healing journey. If you desire to live a life of peace, confidence, and freedom—one that isn't filled with anxiety and fear—then you are in the right place.

We each have a seeker, a dreamer, and a lover inside of us. It's the part of ourselves that we pushed down or tried to forget. The wild and free part that holds our childlike wonder and hope for a life full of meaning, purpose, and fulfillment. Even when we can't feel it, that part is still there, waiting to be given permission to come forward.

But too many of us live in the safe middle and miss out on the inspiring parts of life. The parts of life that light us up and fill our souls. The experiences that we find meaningful and allow us to feel the full range of emotions that life has to offer. Imagine a spectrum where on one end is deep pain and the other end is overwhelming joy. The safe middle is where most of us try to live because it is comfortable and because it allows us to avoid those feelings of pain that are a natural and soul-wrenching part of being human. What we don't realize is that by avoiding that end of the spectrum, we also cut ourselves off from the overwhelming joy. I mean, when's the last time you can say you truly experienced overwhelming joy? The kind that brings you to your knees in gratitude for being alive, fills your eyes with tears, and makes you feel like your heart may explode? In protecting ourselves from the pain, we also keep ourselves from that joy.

I've been that person living in the safe middle. Growing up in a family that struggled with addiction and domestic violence, I learned to operate out of fear and feelings of unworthiness. I carried fear and the pain of my past like a heavy backpack, and it was impacting everything I did without my realizing it. I was afraid to allow myself to be too happy because I was waiting for the other shoe to drop. And I was afraid to allow myself to be fully loved and cared for because I knew that eventually that friendship would end, that relationship might fail, or that person I loved so much would die.

For a long time, I didn't know there was another way of resolving conflict or getting my way other than controlling everything and therefore my own safety or, worse yet, yelling or hitting. Without exposure to the stories and experiences of others, without a willingness to examine and talk about what I experienced growing up, and the patterns of behavior and action that I developed as a result, I never would have come to this awareness. Becoming aware of our beliefs, perceptions, thoughts, and patterns, and exploring why we are the way we are can lead to freedom and peace. Creating this awareness is the first step in a restoration process that can help us be more intentional about the call on our life, the desires of our heart, and the impact we wish to make on the world.

To be restored, we must stop looking for answers outside ourselves and start looking within. We must dig underneath all the layers, labels, pressures, and conditioning. We must ask ourselves deep, reflective questions like: Who am I? What do I believe? Why do I believe what I believe? Why do I think what I think and do what I do? Why do I want what I want? This restoration process opens the door to reaching our potential. We are not going back to a previous version of ourselves, like some definitions of restoration. Instead, we are improved beyond measure.

Through my own restoration process, I have been able to wake up to my own thoughts, behaviors, and choices and free myself of old patterns that hold me back. As I continue to employ the insights, tools, and practices I picked up along the way and share in this book, I am shedding layers of fear and anxiety, despite the curveballs and challenges that life continues to throw at me. I am more resilient and peaceful than ever, and even though some of the most challenging years of my life have happened since my restoration journey began, I still experience more love and joy now than I ever thought possible.

I realized, at some point, that the framework for restoration I'd formed could help others. This is why I founded my company, The Restoration Project.

My colleagues and I believe that people lead from a foundation of who they are, yet most people have never really explored their own identities. Our team sees leadership development as multidimensional and complex, like we are as humans. In a traditional setting, leadership development often starts with training people on skills, but if a person skips straight to building skills, they can overlook or mask some of the patterns and deeper issues that may be getting in the way of being their best as a leader. We prefer to start first with who someone is, what they believe, and what their unique gifts are. We allow people the space to explore their identity and intentions and *then* move into building skills. Starting at this deeper layer unlocks another level of self-awareness, emotional intelligence, compassion, and empathy.

By better understanding who we are, who we are not, what we want, and how people perceive us, each of us can level up our leadership abilities. In walking clients through this restoration process, I have witnessed them get their spark back for life and work. I have seen them break free of the chains of regret and the weight of resentment. I have witnessed them come alive again amid the hope of new possibilities. This is what restoration—being a restored person—looks like.

Contrary to what our culture tries to sell us, there is not one right way to live. There is not one right way to lead. When we try to apply the principles and frameworks that have worked for someone else to our own life and work, and we find that they don't match our values and authentic way of being, we end up achieving and winning but feeling empty. This book will help you reconnect with yourself and the world around you. It will help you restore your deepest intentions and align your life, leadership, and work to that truest and best version of who you are.

This is not a book of answers. Instead, it is a book of questions and frameworks to help you unbecome and unravel the parts of you that are holding you back, so you can become the best version of yourself and fully step into the grandest vision for your life. This book will equip and inspire you to be the unique human you were meant to be. I will be walking alongside you through your own process and sharing insights from my journey to help you find your own way.

It will take time, commitment, and patience to work through this process and achieve a restored existence. It will also take time, commitment, and patience to maintain it. You are being bombarded by messages every day telling you that you are not enough or you don't have enough. Messages that instill fear. Messages of scarcity and lack. To find the truth, you need to dedicate time and effort to filling your mind, heart, and spirit with messages of gratitude and abundance.

If you are dedicated to this process, then you will experience the powerful reality that nothing has to change on the outside for you to be at peace now. To be confident now. To know you are enough. This process is not linear, and it will be ongoing. Life happens. Circumstances change. You change. These concepts, tools, and frameworks will be useful and practical to revisit. They will help you look at things differently and gain clarity. Your mindset, habits, routines, and practices will evolve and continue to do so.

Restoration is a never-ending process. For the rest of your life, you will have to work at this. Same goes for me. I am a fellow traveler on the journey. I don't know it all, but I do know that wholeness, freedom, and peace are worth pursuing even if we never quite grasp them. We must continue to connect, reflect, learn, and grow until the day we leave this earth. It isn't neat and tidy, and it isn't comfortable. Trust that even when you aren't seeing or feeling changes, just by walking the path and going through this restoration process, change and transformation *are* happening. As I provide examples and paths, it's important you listen to yourself and take the steps that feel right to you. Your way is the right one.

Challenge yourself to reconnect with your inner voice and inner knowing. Quiet the external noise. You will know you are on the right path when peace, confidence, and freedom settle into your life, leadership, and work for longer and longer periods of time. Events and circumstances will come up that knock us off kilter like a job change, a natural disaster, a sudden loss, or an illness. In those times, we may need to invest more time and effort to bring ourselves back to a place of being centered and grounded. If at any point you feel stuck, you may want to reach out to our team or another coach, mentor, counselor, or healer to help. Another person can help you get unstuck and accelerate your growth.

As a restored human and leader, you will hear people describe you as some or all of the following:

aware	kind	honorable
present	patient	cheerful
curious	gentle	lighthearted
clear	positive	expansive
confident	generous	composed
compassionate	considerate	undisturbed
courageous	stable	friendly
open	grounded	gracious
honest	disciplined	merciful
connected	steady	true
calm	poised	understanding
committed	dignified	brave

I've seen it countless times. And you will move closer to the ability to develop an inspiring vision, set quality goals and priorities, manage stress, overcome failure, forgive, listen well, better understand yourself and others, invite in differences, navigate change, manage conflict, provide an opinion and stay open, communicate more clearly, and more.

There is something you have to keep in mind as you dive into this work: This book is for you and the work is yours to do, but it's ultimately not about you. We were put on this earth to love and be loved. We were meant to lead and work and serve. To do that well, we have to work on ourselves first to become restored, healthy, and whole. After we have established safety, trust, connection, and belonging in our own lives, only then can we provide that to others.

For example, when I'm having coffee with a friend and I'm fully connected, I am noticing the energy between us and listening intently to the language they are using, and I take longer pauses to really hear and consider what is being said and how I feel. If I'm on a walk, I am noticing the birds, the color of the trees, how the breeze feels on my skin, and how my body feels. It's a full sensory experience. In everyday moments, I know I'm connected when I can experience these mundane, everyday tasks as if I were a third-party observer, seeing things as if I'm outside of it, looking in, and fully aware of all the sights, smells, and feelings of that moment in time. Many of us experience this level of awareness when we have a big experience or are on vacation and completely able to unplug and be present. But this level of awareness is available to us all the time if we choose it; if we slow down a bit, get intentional about bringing our focus to the here and now, and eliminate distractions or train our mind not to wander.

For many of us, we haven't felt this level of connection since we were kids. Let's start with small steps. Where can you find the time and place in your day to be alone in the quiet? Many of my clients are working moms and their only option is a few minutes of time in their car before they go into the office or into the house. That's a place to start. If you aren't ready to be completely still yet, maybe during your walk or workout, you go in silence instead of filling the void with a podcast, audiobook, or music. Or you could simply turn off the radio while driving. These aren't full presence and engagement, but they're a step in the right direction toward the silence and stillness that will allow for connection.

When you are in this space, just start to notice how you're feeling—physically, mentally, emotionally, spiritually. What are you thinking about? What are you worried about? Creating space to become aware of your thoughts and feelings is the point of rebuilding connection. From this place you can honestly explore and examine who you are and why you are the way you are. Some of the answers you are looking for are buried deep. You have to create space for them to come to the surface. They may come into your mind or your heart in a way you don't understand or can't comprehend right away. Don't worry! You will get there one step at a time.

Try this reconnection exercise with me. Find a quiet place where you can be alone and uninterrupted. When you are in this quiet space alone, find a comfortable position and close your eyes. You are going to start with breathing. Take a deep breath in slowly through the nose and out slowly through your mouth. Do this five times. You can put your hand over your heart, if you wish. This is something I love to do.

This intentional breathing brings you fully into the present moment and allows you to reconnect with your body, your heart, and your spirit. Feel this connection. If you've never done this before, you will likely feel vulnerable and emotional. If you experience these feelings, you are on the right path. That tender part of you, likely yourself as a small child before you closed yourself off from others and shut down your hopes and dreams—that's the part of yourself that you are trying to reconnect with. Full connection will feel like all the parts of yourself that have been bustling about in the day are pulling back into your body.

When you feel that connection, you are ready to explore the questions offered in the exercises within this book. Fair warning: For those who are not comfortable with stillness and silence, this will be very challenging, and it may take a long time. Don't beat yourself up, and take a break if you're getting frustrated, but continue to practice. Trust me, it took me a long time to quiet the noise and let go. As you get some practice, you'll be able to notice your level of connection and whether you are open or closed in real time.

Are you feeling it? At least a little? Once you've had some practice clearing the way for silence and stillness, I'd like you to try the following exercise.

THE DUMPING EXERCISE

This is one of my favorite exercises of all time, and I use it often. When my schedule is full and there's a lot happening, I may do it once a day or multiple times per week. When things are less busy, I do it once a week or at least once per month. The dumping exercise helps me regroup and refocus my time and energy on the right things. We all get out of whack, so it has become a critical practice in my life.

It is also a great exercise to use anytime you are feeling overwhelmed or anxious. Getting things down on paper can make all the difference. Science tells us that when we take things swirling in our head and physically write them down so we can see them, we regain a sense of control and can move forward with more clarity and confidence.

Take out a sheet of paper, and while you are fully present and engaged, pour out whatever comes up for each of the following questions:

- What is on your heart?
- What is on your mind?
- What is on your to-do list?

Don't overthink it. When it comes out, write it down. Some things may not make sense or may surprise you. That's when you know you're doing it right! There is no correct order. Just start with the list that comes to you first. I'm usually in my head more than my heart, so I have to dump out my to-do list and what's on my mind before I can get to what's on my heart.

You might be wondering what types of things could be in each of these buckets. Fair question, as you are not yet comfortable with freely writing out anything that comes up or may be subconsciously resisting this exercise. Things on your heart may be what you care about, something that's troubling you, a

continued

hurt you're carrying, people you are thinking of. Things on your mind may include your worries, fears, anxieties, and things you wish you could change. Things on your to-do list are pretty self-explanatory. Now, give yourself some time and start writing!

Once you have your lists or one big list, review what you've written down and take the following steps:

1. Cross off what isn't yours to carry.
2. Assign "delete," "delegate," or "defer" labels to the remainder.
3. Prioritize what's left of the list.
4. Assign dates and take action.

If you're honest with yourself, there will always be circumstances, to-dos, worries, emotions, and even people on your lists that aren't yours to carry because you can't control them or aren't responsible for them. My clients are typically shocked when they see the number of items on their lists that are taking up their energy but aren't their burdens to carry. No wonder we feel depleted!

Once you have those first items crossed off, review the rest for things you can delete, delegate, or defer. Write names or dates by those that can be delegated or deferred. Next, take what's left, which will be your to-dos, and prioritize them. Finally, assign dates to complete the to-dos and take the list with you to get back into action.

How do you feel? I know each time I do this, I am surprised by how relieved and clear I feel compared to how anxious and uncertain I felt going in. It's so simple, yet so powerful. Use the dumping exercise as often as feels right to you. Not only does it add a little silence and stillness to your day, but it's another great way to rebuild connection with yourself and increase your self-awareness and understanding. You'll be surprised by all that you learn about yourself as you continue to practice this exercise!

To help you on your journey, I've divided the book into three parts:

Part 1: Rebuilding Connection, will walk you through how to rebuild connection with yourself and the world around you. You will explore your identity and reflect on the experiences and influences from your past and in your life that have shaped your thoughts, beliefs, actions, and patterns. Then, through surrender, forgiveness, and other practices, you'll invite in perspective, evaluate the meaning of it all, and release what is no longer serving you.

In **Part 2: Restoring Intention,** you will restore intention by exploring what is meaningful and valuable to you, envisioning what's possible, asking for input, and learning new ways forward.

And in **Part 3: Aligning Action,** you will align your actions with what you discovered in Part 1 and what you explored in Part 2. You will then be able to determine what needs to change and what can't change, develop an action plan, invite in support, integrate and assess as you try new things, and wrap up with the final and most important step: share what you've learned with others.

Remember, this is a circular process that you can pick up and continue time and time again as you move through your life, leadership, and working journey. And the more people who use this process, the more positive change we will continue to see in our families, workplaces, communities, and world!

I have been actively using these questions and frameworks in my own life for over ten years, and in my practice, my colleagues and I have had the honor of walking alongside hundreds of leaders across the world as they work through their own restoration process and commit to living and leading with more intention. I hope you experience the same reinvigorating excitement and fulfillment in your life and work as they have.

Turn the page, and let's get started.

PART 1

Rebuilding Connection

Understanding yourself or someone else in a real way requires connection. Most of us have experienced surface-level connection or even transactional connection, but here I am talking about something much deeper and more intimate. A real heart connection. We have to experience this connection first with ourselves, and eventually we can extend this type of connection to others.

Have you ever really looked at yourself in the mirror? I mean stared into your own eyes, the windows to your soul, to try and see yourself for who you really are? How about sitting across from someone and staring into their eyes without saying a word? I challenge you to try it. It's uncomfortable! It makes us feel really vulnerable and exposed, which is why we don't do it. That vulnerability, that level of connection, that's what's required for you to start this process. You have to be willing to see yourself for who you really are, all of you—which means accepting the beautiful parts and the ugly parts because we all have them.

Allow yourself as you read this book to connect with your mind, heart, body, and soul in a way you likely never have before. Cut the noise. Focus. Go deeper. Especially in this first part of the framework, you will need silence, stillness, and the courage to do some honest self-reflection. As the layers shed and the things you've carried and buried are exposed, I will show you how to sprinkle in self-care and celebration practices to bring you back to the truth of who you were meant to be: someone who is hopeful, joyful, and peaceful, able to operate at your best.

We are all significant in our own way, and it's up to each of us to find our own path, create our own story, and build our own life. Connection is the key. To move from unawareness to some level of awareness about anything is one of the most challenging parts of being human. It's the reason so many of us never embark on this journey. We are simply unaware that we are unaware. Like a fish, we don't realize we are in the water, and we know no other way except to swim—and we don't know that we even know how! Maybe another example is breathing. We do it without thinking about it, but we are able to become aware of *how* we are doing it when someone explains the process of breathing and how we can witness it. In mindfulness and meditation practices, we are invited to shut our eyes, quiet our minds, and bring our focus to our breath. Feel our chest rise and fall. Some practices invite us to take breaths on a count—count to four as you breathe in and count to four as you breathe out. This helps us become aware of what we typically take for granted because it often happens without us thinking about it. Like breathing, many of our thoughts, beliefs, and actions are so hardwired that we aren't aware of them. This book will challenge you to become aware of them and to examine them. Be gentle with yourself. Feelings of frustration and shame may come up as you increase your awareness. You take this step honoring what has been and remaining hopeful for what will be.

Doing the work of rebuilding connection can be difficult, but it is required if you want to live a truly meaningful life and do fulfilling work. The insights and exercises in Part 1 and throughout the book are for those who are bold and audacious enough to desire the most out of life. As you face fears and experiences that you would rather ignore, it's important to remember that when you ignore these things, they don't actually go away. You carry them within yourself where they influence your thoughts, feelings, perceptions, outlook, and actions. But when you have the courage to face and process these fears, you set yourself free of the burden they once were. You just have to allow yourself to gently push past the initial fear you feel and recognize that when you come out on the other side, you'll be stronger, ready, resilient, *restored*.

For many of you, reading this triggers a deep knowing. For others, you may think it sounds absurd. You may even be angered by what I've said so far. Know that these are all normal reactions. As humans, we don't like anything that questions our ideals or challenges us to change. This is what keeps us stuck, what keeps us captive. We get uncomfortable and avoid our fears and feelings instead of facing them head on, acknowledging and accepting them so we can be free.

Many of my clients have been completely unaware of the subconscious narratives that were shaping their lives and leadership and ultimately holding them back. They've learned to operate through their entire lives like this, not realizing they could experience a freedom and release that would allow them to maximize their potential and achieve more fulfillment, purpose, and joy in life. This is why rebuilding connection is so important. No matter who you are or where you are as you read this, you will gain insights and ideas that will positively impact your life, leadership, work, and relationships.

So how do you reconnect with yourself and your identity? You have to make time and space. In this part of the book, you will learn practices and techniques for breaking yourself out of autopilot and reactivity to make room for increased awareness and intentionality. You will explore the thoughts you think, the feelings you have, the experiences you've been through, and the influences and patterns that have shaped your life. You will invite in additional people and perspectives to help you see and understand things in a different way. Multiple voices are always better than one, and because you can't see your own blind spots, it's important that you invite those you trust and admire to share their perceptions of what you are exploring.

Part 1 of this journey is the steepest and most challenging part. But as you round out this part, you will begin to make sense of and search for meaning in all you have discovered. There will be things you will need to unlearn and things you will need to let go of, surrender, and release before you can move on. Depending on when you are reading this book in your life journey, you may have more layers, experiences, beliefs, and patterns to evaluate. You may even find yourself questioning the foundation upon which you have built your identity.

There will be ideas, beliefs, and parts of yourself that have to fall away to make room for the truth and something greater. If you find yourself resisting here, come back to your heart and to that deeper sense of connection. Your mind may want to resist while your heart is calling you to something new. This is a natural part of the process. The process will refine you, strengthen you, and build long-term resilience if you can move yourself out of your comfort zone and through the resistance into exploration and eventually acceptance.

As you move through this important work, know that everything does not have to be evaluated all at once. As I said before, this is a life-long journey. Feel your way through the process, reflect, revisit, and give yourself grace. You will know when you are ready to move to the second part of the journey. Beginning to listen to and trust yourself again is a beautiful relearning that happens in all of this.

Discovering and then releasing what no longer serves us is a critical part of our personal evolution as a human and a leader that we typically avoid or skip. We like to jump straight to dreaming and doing more, likely because letting go can be painful. When we succumb to the temptation of skipping this part or moving through it too quickly, we find ourselves unsettled, frustrated, anxious, and eventually back at the base of the mountain, having taken the wrong path . . . again.

But I've found that the fastest way to where we are headed is through the pain and some of the things we have avoided. You will encounter periods of darkness and struggle. You will wonder why you are doing this and if it's working. But if you avoid these struggles instead of accepting and moving through them, you won't be able to get to the right path. You will continue to end up stuck and struggling, prolonging your journey to freedom and peace. As much as possible, be open to the process, and you'll find that, all at once, things will come together, and you'll be transformed. I promise. Make your way at your own pace, resting and filling up when you need to. Here we go!

CHAPTER 1

Reconnecting with Yourself and Your Identity

How are you feeling? What are you thinking? What do you want? If you feel restless and unsettled when faced with these questions, then settle in with me here. Most of us are moving through life completely disconnected—from ourselves, from others, from everything around us—and we don't even realize it. Many of my clients have no idea where to start when I ask them those three questions in our first few visits. Life is noisy and busy. We are moving so quickly from one thing to the next that before we know it, our mind feels like a jumbled mess. We've long forgotten what we want because we are reacting to whatever comes at us. We become so used to the frantic pace that moments of silence and stillness make us uneasy.

Well, the hard truth is that reconnection requires us to slow down. It's uncomfortable for most and even painful for some. That's OK! When all we've ever known is busy and noisy, when it has become our default, what else could we expect? At a young age and for a thousand different reasons, we learned that disconnection was easier and safer. Thinking too much and feeling too much was not OK. Being in a close relationship ended in us getting hurt. So we slowly started erecting our walls, putting on armor, and staying busy to avoid ourselves and others from connecting in a real way.

When I started my own restoration process, my calendar was maxed out. My husband used to tease me for my inability to sit still through a full episode of *Law & Order*, and my friends would comment on my inability to make it through and enjoy a card game. If it didn't serve a purpose or I couldn't win at it, I didn't see the point. I was so focused on getting things done in that phase of my life that I was completely disconnected from myself and everyone around me and, most of the time, even from the task I was completing. I was simply checking the box and going through the motions while my mind was already on to the next thing.

I had to learn how to come back to myself and remember what connection feels like. To help you do the same, I am going to give you some exercises and questions in this chapter, but before you get to the *doing*, you will have to work on the *being*. The quality of your answers will be proportional to how connected you are in the moment you are answering them.

In its simplest form, connection is full presence and engagement. It's what we experience when our heart, mind, body, and spirit are together and fully focused on where we are and what we are doing in the present moment. Can you remember what that feels like? I experience this connection when I allow an experience to overtake me. My mind isn't thinking about what was or what could be, but is fully engaged in the here and now. My heart is open and I am fully aware of how I'm feeling in that moment. All of my senses are engaged and I'm in tune with the sights, smells, and other sensory experiences around me. I feel settled and at the same time fully engaged and alive.

WHY RECONNECTING IS IMPORTANT

We are working on rebuilding connection, increasing our awareness, and waking up proactively because the risk is that we stay asleep until something terrible happens. For most of us, it is a difficulty or tragedy in our life that forces us to wake up and reconnect with ourselves. In my own life, I had two wake-up calls that started to bring about the awareness that I was disconnected from myself and the world around me.

The first experience occurred during a trip to New York City in my late twenties. In that period of my life, I was enjoying the fruits of what culture would say was a successful life. I had a flourishing career, a great partner, lots of friends, invites to all the parties, money, status—more than my small-town dreams could have ever wished for. Then, one summer, I traveled extensively all around the country on back-to-back trips for work. I remember waking up in my hotel room in Manhattan one morning, looking out the window at the hustle and bustle of the most populated city in America and suddenly realizing how deeply lonely I felt. That soul-shaking loneliness brought a sudden flood of tears I couldn't stop. This feeling and the tears surprised me. I'd built the future I wanted and achieved what I set out to do. So where was all this coming from? My typical response in moments like this was to shove those feelings aside or bury them down deep—to leave them unexplored for fear of where they would take me.

I knew, on some level, I had been feeling this way for months before that morning, and the restlessness and loneliness had kept growing. That morning, I allowed myself to let them in. I sat in my thoughts and feelings and examined them with compassion and curiosity. I journaled on what had happened to bring them here and what they were telling me. I felt raw, open, and vulnerable, but I couldn't shake those feelings. Over time, I continued to wrestle with them, even talking with trusted friends and loved ones about them, and exploring them with my then-therapist and coach. In allowing myself to dwell in this space, I found some answers, many that calmed me and a few that scared me.

I came to realize that I was lonely because I spent most of my time in surface-level conversation when I actually craved deep, meaningful connection and friendships. The way I had designed my life up to that point didn't allow for what I truly wanted and needed as a human being. I also didn't like big cities, and although the glamorous restaurants and experiences were nice, they weren't for me. I endured them, but I didn't enjoy them. I realized and made peace with the fact that I was a small-town girl who didn't really mesh with the big city lifestyle, and I came to the understanding that this was OK with me.

The biggest discovery that drove me deeper into reconnection with myself was the realization that I had been chasing the dreams and climbing the ladders that other people set up for me. When I was asked why I was doing all of this, I didn't have a good answer. I was doing it because I thought that's what I was supposed to do—because that's what others expected of me and because the money and the status and all those other things would make me happy. But the reality was that they didn't, and they wouldn't. I recognized that for me to be able to be at peace with myself and pursue what was important to me, some things would have to change. I had to create my own definition of success.

My definition of success turned out to be undefined and unexplored, and I came to realize my definition wasn't the same one that society and others around me had. It was much later and after several more experiences that I discovered some key questions that could have helped me avoid a few more mistaken routes on my own journey. I asked myself what a good life would look like if I were to change things and what ultimately mattered to me. And I also thought about what I might do if I weren't tied to financial constraints. These wound up being life-changing questions for me.

CREATING OR REFINING YOUR DEFINITION OF SUCCESS

If you're ready, I'd like you to take some time to explore these same questions:

- What does a good life look like for you?
- What will matter in the end?
- What would you do if money wasn't a factor?

You can write down your thoughts, feelings, and answers to the questions, or you can simply explore them in your head. Know that your answers can and will change over time because you change and the circumstances of your life change. Remember that you have a choice to leave the guilt and shame behind as new things are revealed to you. Coming to these realizations can be difficult, but I truly believe it's better late than never. As you explore these questions, keep in mind that your answers don't have to make sense. Let the first thing that comes to mind out.

WHY WE RESIST CONNECTING

When I first asked myself what I would do if money didn't matter, my answer surprised me. I blurted out that I wanted to be a pastor! I resisted and wanted to take back that response almost as soon as it came out because I could see that it was the complete opposite of how I was living and working at the time. But I knew I had begun a journey, so instead of discounting my answer, I sat with it and pondered it for a long while. What about being a pastor appealed to me? What changes would be required to even make that a reality? I came to some wonderful and beautiful realizations in having the courage to explore that answer. And no, I am not a pastor today in the traditional sense of that word and occupation. Just because you say something out loud, or come to realize something, doesn't mean you have to act on it or that it will become your reality. Simply allow yourself the freedom to explore.

To reconnect with your full self and get to a place where your ego is out of the way and you are speaking truth from your heart, there are additional steps you have to take. When you start your exploration of these questions, you will come up with surface-level answers. That's OK, but you don't want to stop there. You want to continue to explore and let your answers get deeper. If you're willing, revisit the three questions we just walked through to allow yourself to expand your exploration and answers.

GOING DEEPER WITH YOUR DEFINITION OF SUCCESS

This is a chance for you to go deeper and ask yourself:

What does a good life look like for you?
In considering what a good life looks like for you, allow yourself to envision and explore what you are doing, how you are feeling, and what is happening around you. What do these answers reveal to you? What do they mean?

What will matter in the end?
Allow yourself to move to the end of your life. Yes, that is scary. We spend much of our time avoiding the fact that one day our

life will be over. This tricks us into thinking we will have more time to make the changes we should make today. Many people get to the end of their life with regret because they will not allow themselves to connect with the deepest truths inside them and explore this question honestly. They will not allow themselves to face death. I hope you will not let that be you. Allow the answers to come. Do not judge your feelings and responses. Just be with them.

What would you do if money wasn't a factor?
Allow yourself to set aside the realities of life and explore this question openly. There are a million reasons why you may not be able to fully live the answer to this question because—let's face it—money does matter. Each of us has responsibilities and needs. Push past that resistance and let the answers come. What do the answers show you about what you want and what matters to you? What do they reveal about what you care about and how you want to be of service to the world?

You don't need to *do* anything with what you just learned, but you can if you want to. This exercise is about reconnecting to that part of yourself that you have numbed out, disconnected from, or shut down. It's about remembering who you were before all the self-protection. Letting that part of yourself come back to life—reigniting that light—is an important part of the restoration process and becoming whole again.

Self-protection is a normal part of life. When difficult things happen around us or to us, we decide not to talk about it. We keep ourselves busy so we don't have to think about it. Maybe we even deny it ever happened. We convince ourselves that avoiding it altogether would keep us from feeling the pain of it. We stuff our thoughts and feelings. We get good at carrying and burying. When we are told that our hopes and dreams are not possible, we stop sharing what we hoped for and quit dreaming. We keep those hopes and dreams locked inside until it is too painful to live with them, and then we kill them off and conform.

This happens to all of us, one small incident at a time. We settle into a mediocre existence of consuming and reacting. This becomes our reality with little awareness. We experience some restlessness and discontent but convince ourselves to ignore it, and we stay stuck in the mundane. Suffocated. Suffering in silence. We protect ourselves from anything that might challenge our thoughts or feelings because it is too painful.

Out of that sense of protection, we lose our ability to hold opposites or see both sides. We take extreme positions on things and feel defensive most of the time. We feel a need to protect and hide things. We won't allow ourselves to be vulnerable. We don't trust ourselves. We don't trust anyone else. We hold ourselves back from loving or receiving love. These are signs of disconnection. This is a signal that we need restoration.

My Second Opportunity to Wake Up and Connect

My second awakening that helped me fully embrace and surrender to the restoration process was when my boyfriend-now-husband (thank you, God!) told me our relationship could go no further because I would never trust him. Every fiber of my being inflamed in that moment. I became outraged and irrational. Yelling, screaming, blaming, and pushing him away. In the days following that ugly experience, those words would not leave my head. "You will never trust me."

I knew deep down that was the truth, but I wasn't ready to take responsibility for what it meant. Honestly, I didn't know how to take responsibility for it because I hadn't trusted anyone, including myself, for as long as I could remember, and I had assumed that was just how it would be until the end. I had adapted to the endings of friendships and relationships when people got too close or something happened as a result of my distrust. It was easy to blame them and move on to someone new. But I didn't want to move on from Mitch. I wanted to be with him, and it was clear that I couldn't be with him if I followed the same patterns I had up to that point. There were truths about myself and my life I had been avoiding, and that had to end if there was to be any chance we would be together.

I dove back into therapy and other healing modalities and discovered a lot about myself. Looking back, I wish I had already developed the tools and thinking to be able to reconnect with the truth of my identity at the time. It took a lot of soul-searching, questioning, mental toughness, and courage, but I was committed to doing what I needed to do to bring about the change I hoped for. Among other things, I thought about situations in my life when I had not kept my promises, when I was not operating with the kind of integrity I wanted, when I told myself half-truths. And I explored who I was beneath all the labels others imposed on me and that I applied to myself.

THE NEXT LEVEL OF AWARENESS

Let's unlock another level of awareness and connection by diving into those four situations: not keeping promises, not operating with integrity, not telling yourself the whole truth, and trying to discover who you are underneath the labels. First, frame these scenarios as questions (see the following). Some may be difficult to answer, but take your time. This is new territory. Sit with

continued

each question for a while and allow more answers to come. When you get an answer, try to go deeper. Consider revisiting these questions over a few days or weeks to see how your answers evolve, and remember to use your reconnection routine! Ask yourself:

Where in your life have you not kept your promises?

This is a great question to get you thinking about the dreams you have given up on or the ways you have compromised what you wanted in place of what others expected of you. It's a great reconnection question. Please give yourself grace and allow any shame or guilt from the answers to leave you. You are here now. You are creating awareness now. You are reestablishing a connection to live with more intention. That is amazing!

Where are you out of your integrity?

We can compromise our integrity and break trust with ourselves and others in both big and small ways. When you are out of your integrity, you don't feel whole and may feel as if something is missing. Be open as you explore. Get curious.

Where are you not telling the full truth?

This question gets you thinking about where you are not being honest and true with yourself and others. Again, with this question, you are attempting to create awareness of your own desires, wants, and needs. Drop any negative feelings that come up and free yourself to focus forward.

Who are you beneath all the labels?

We all have roles that we play and labels that define us: son, daughter, friend, employee, mother, father, wife, husband, hard worker, loyal partner, helper, leader, etc. Beneath all of that, what is your true essence? What is at the core of your identity? This can be a hard concept to grasp. If we strip all those surface-level labels away, who are you?

LIVING WITH MEANING AND INTENTION BEYOND THE LABELS

Reconnecting with ourselves and our identity allows us to live a life of purpose. It gives us our power back to choose. Whether we realize it or not, our energy, ideas, thoughts, feelings, and everything in between impact our daily life, those around us, and the world at large. We can waste our opportunity or let it happen by accident. Or we can invest some time and energy to grow our awareness and be more intentional.

When we grow our awareness, we increase the depth and richness of our relationships and experiences. We empower ourselves out of a victim mentality. We reignite the spark inside us that brings passion and meaning back into our life. Becoming aware and reconnecting is the first step toward unlocking answers. It allows us to unravel what has confined us, so we can unleash our full potential.

Stepping outside of all the labels can be challenging to do. They have been the foundation of our life, and they are important to us. They give us parameters by which we can make decisions and feel like we fit in. All of that is great until one of those labels is taken away from us. We lose a job, lose a parent, lose a child—and then we lose our center. We start to believe that we are nothing because we no longer have that one label attached to us. I have witnessed this time and time again with clients. You are so much more than one thing, but in order to know that and believe it, you have to think about it well in advance of it being taken from you.

If you have a hard time considering how to move past those roles and labels to define who you are, it could be helpful to consider what you care about. The next two questions we will explore may be helpful in finding answers that aren't so dependent on other people or a particular circumstance. The first is asking what things you consider to be important or valuable. For instance, being in nature and having alone time are important to me. Spending quality time with my husband is also meaningful and valuable to me. These activities leave me feeling restored, connected, grounded, and loved. To live these out, I would identify myself as "a nature lover," "independent," "adventurous," "caring," and "loving." I would prioritize my time and energy accordingly, making time for these activities and prioritizing them on my calendar.

The second question to help you move beyond traditional labels is asking what your personal core values are. These values help you root yourself in words that describe who you are and what you care about. We all have them whether we realize it or not. They impact the way we see the world and what we believe. It's powerful to bring them to our awareness. For instance, if integrity is a core value for you, then you get very upset and offended when people lie, cheat, or steal. It's important to explore what these words mean to you because words mean different things to different people.

Early in my practice, I had clients who were in conflict, and I knew it would be helpful to bring them together around core values to reestablish connection and understanding. Each of them named respect as a core value. However, the meaning of the word was different for each of them. Person 1 said that respect meant to them that you always follow through on what you say you will do. Person 2 believed respect meant you are nice to others. Person 2 often did not follow through on what they said they were going to do, and person 1 was very direct and honest about their disappointment when that happened. You could see how they were in a vicious circle of misunderstanding. Bringing this to their awareness helped them work better together.

My own core values are love, courage, and intention. In describing myself as loving, courageous, and intentional, I'm compelled to think about what these mean and what they should look like. What does a loving person do? How do I know I am loving? What would a loving person do in this situation? You get the idea. Over time, these values positively impact the thoughts I think, the words I use, and the actions I take. When I get stressed or out of alignment, I can focus on them to bring myself back to the best version of me.

YOUR CORE VALUES

Let's make some time for you to explore what's meaningful and valuable to you and to think about your core values. Keep in mind, these can change over time, as different seasons of life can change your answers. If you've never explored these questions before, you may need to give yourself time and space to explore them over and over until the answers "feel" right to you. Allow yourself to move out of your head. You don't need to justify your answers. Your answers don't need to make logical sense. Simply trust your heart and your gut. Ask yourself:

What is meaningful and valuable to you?
Consider where you spend your time, energy, and money. Think about what you believe is important, and compile your list.

What values do you hold close?
Many of us hold virtues or values, such as respect, integrity, honesty, loyalty, courage, and love, close to us. What are your top two or three values? Write down what they mean to you in one to two sentences.

REMEMBERING WHO WE ARE

You've done some big work in this chapter. You've likely discovered some new things and remembered many things. Much of our work together is about remembering who we are in our truest form, our deepest identity, the one who has always been there. These crucial parts of ourselves get covered up by the noise of life until we sometimes don't even realize they exist anymore. Layers and layers get put on top of that bright light in us that is our nature. We add some on ourselves to conform or fit in, and others put layers on us through their expectations of and desires for us. It's our job to peel each of those layers back until we have remembered the truth of who we are. When we know, love, and respect who we really are, we no longer feel the need to hide, pretend, or please. We can be who we are in all situations.

As we move through this process together, I will end each chapter with the same questions you'll see following this paragraph. This is because reflection and integration are an important part of this journey. Making time to revisit what you are exploring, discovering, learning, remembering, surrendering, and releasing helps you see progress, so you're motivated to keep going. I also want to be sure, like with all my clients, that you are *doing* something about what you are learning. Change and transformation don't happen without action. You need to commit to being or doing something different. Be honest and commit, my friend. I recommend writing out the answers to these questions because seeing them in black and white is powerful. But if nothing else, please sit with them and let the answers come to you!

REFLECT ON YOUR JOURNEY

- What have you learned, unlearned, or relearned in this chapter?
- What has been most valuable to you?
- What one thing will you commit to doing differently going forward?
- Who can you invite in to keep you accountable?

CHAPTER 2

Reflecting on Experiences, Beliefs, and Behaviors

I took a writing class one winter. There were eight of us in the class, and we met after dark in a big, beautiful, old house. It was a safe and cozy place where we explored several forms of writing, including how writing can help us heal. In one class, we were asked to think about a very difficult time in our lives, then to close our eyes, picture ourselves there, and allow ourselves to become aware of what that memory did to our body. After a while, we were prompted to write about it and told we would eventually share this memory with the rest of the class.

I took myself back to my early teen years when my sister, stepsister, and I witnessed a violent fight between my dad and stepmom. Following the incident, I was in therapy off and on for years, well into my adult life, and this particular experience served as the topic of many of those therapy sessions. I thought for sure I had already processed my way through it, so what happened in my writing class was completely unexpected.

As I sat with my eyes closed, fully immersed in that memory, I was overcome with fear and overwhelmed by pain. My entire body got hot and sweaty, my chest felt heavy, and my heartbeat quickened. My throat tightened, I felt sick to my stomach, and the tears began to flow. I was so uncomfortable that I thought I might have to leave the room. Needless to say, I could hardly get a word out when it was time to share, and I stayed after our class to visit with the healer who had led the session to understand what had happened. She explained to me that sometimes what we have worked through in our minds is still carried within our body, and we have healing to do in a different way to continue to release that experience. I was intrigued and started this new healing journey with her.

During our time together, I learned how most of my beliefs, thoughts, actions, and choices had been shaped by my experiences when I was young. Growing up around abuse, I held a core belief that *I was not safe*. In fact, that became my default setting. I came to understand that my nervous system had been and still was in fight-or-flight mode most of the time, even though so many years had passed and I'd thought I was doing pretty OK in life. I realized this was one explanation for why I always had a hard time getting comfortable or settling down anywhere.

I also learned that because I was hurt by people close to me, I developed a core belief that if I could not trust them, *I could not trust anyone*. I recalled that when I reacted strongly to what was happening in my environment, I was told I was overreacting or being foolish and so I then developed a belief that *I couldn't trust myself or my own intuition*. And out of my early experiences, I arrived at two additional core beliefs that developed into patterns of thought and behavior that I could see had informed me throughout my life: *I was not worthy*, and *it was my job to rescue and protect others*. These core beliefs have played out in a number of ways that have kept me from being healthy and whole—ways I only started to realize in my late twenties and continue to unravel today:

- Believing I am not safe has shown up in many ways in my life, including my scarcity mindset around money, defensiveness when someone gives me feedback, and overreaction to behaviors I perceive as threats at home and in the workplace.

- Believing I can't trust anyone or myself has negatively impacted my relationships in all aspects of life and work. My friendships remained surface level for a long time because I was unwilling to let people know the real me. My marriage suffered because I wouldn't allow myself to receive love from my husband, which left me in lack and him feeling rejected. My leadership also suffered because I didn't ask for help, pretended to know all the answers, and wouldn't trust others to do what I delegated to them.

- Believing I am broken had me stuck in a loop of self-sabotage that I am only now starting to understand. Whenever things got good in my life, I would often do something to wreck it because deep down I didn't feel like I deserved it.

- Believing I have to rescue and protect others still has a firm grip on me that has me regularly overstepping and swooping in to help where I am not needed, only to find myself exhausted and resentful because I'm trying to help where it isn't my job to.

I share this about me in the hope that it helps you start to understand yourself a little better. As we move forward through this book, we will discuss how to remove or better manage these fears and limiting beliefs. But for now, your job is to simply explore and discover. Let go of and lay down any anger, shame, or resentment that comes up.

THE POWER OF REFLECTION

What experiences have shaped your life? Writing helps us process, so now it's your turn to try this journaling exercise. No judgment, just open exploration. No one has to see what you write down, and there is nothing you have to do about what you find. If it worries you, you can burn or shred your paper right after you're done!

It's also important to note that when we have had perfectly good life experiences, there are still little papercut experiences that impact our beliefs and behaviors in ways that go unnoticed. Even if we had the best parents and teachers, there are things that were said and done that we perceived and received a certain way. We are not blaming anyone for this; we are simply creating awareness of our feelings and experience, so we see the truth in it and free ourselves from any limits that experience may have put on us.

To get started, grab your journal and find a quiet space. Remember, you want to allow the answers to come from your heart. Before you dive in, remember to reconnect with your body and your heart by placing your hand over your heart and taking four to five slow, deep breaths. This will help you calm your mind and get present. As you ask yourself each question, accept whatever comes up without judgment or resistance. Write it down. Give yourself time. Multiple answers may come. Challenge yourself to go deeper and explore beyond the initial answer. Don't overthink it. Allow it to flow and see what you find.

Consider the best experiences of your life, the most challenging ones, and random memories that are as vivid as yesterday. Make your list and then explore these additional questions:

- How did these experiences make you feel?
- What were you believing as they happened?

- What are some common emotions and behaviors that show up in your life?

Think about what emotions you often name when someone asks you how you are feeling. Many of us have a small emotional vocabulary. We may only be able to name the very basic emotions of happy, sad, and angry. If this is true for you, find a resource (you can search for "list of emotions" or "emotional language descriptions") that allows you to explore some other emotions and their meanings as you make your list. Once you have it, then explore the following questions:

- What could this emotion mean?
- Where might these emotions have originated?
- What beliefs do you hold true about yourself?

When you think about who you are and what you believe to be true about yourself, what comes to mind? Think about the good and the not-so-good. Write them down and then consider the following:

- Where could these beliefs have originated?
- What patterns and habits have these created in your life?
- What beliefs do you hold true about others and the world?

What are some general statements you make about other people? Please also openly and honestly explore any biases or stereotypes you hold. What do you believe to be true about the world? As you write down you answers, go deeper and consider:

- Where could these beliefs have originated?
- What patterns and habits have these created in your life?

THE CHALLENGE OF DEEPENING OUR AWARENESS

As you move through the process of deepening your connection and awareness, it is important to keep in mind that much of what you have been avoiding or ignoring will come to the surface. This can be difficult and even scary, but you need to let it happen. Understanding that you are a neutral bystander separate from your thoughts and feelings can help you to hold them with curiosity and compassion and not get caught up in them. You are not your thoughts—they are things to be examined and challenged.

As you reconnect with yourself and become aware of the ways you may not be in alignment, it's normal to start to wonder why. This is why we explore how our beliefs, thoughts, and behaviors have been formed. We perceive the world through a lens rooted in what we have experienced. Those experiences shape who we become in many ways.

They also create beliefs, thoughts, and behavior patterns that are rooted in fear and untruths that can hold us back if they go unexamined. Just as a fish doesn't realize it lives in water, we often remain unaware that our beliefs, thoughts, and behaviors are our choice. We do not have to be a product of what we have done or what has been done to us, and we are able to change. In fact, we were born to change, but we can't change if we aren't willing to figure out where we are and where we want to go.

FEAR AND LIMITING BELIEFS

All of us, to some extent, think and act out of fear and limiting beliefs. Limiting beliefs are simply false beliefs about ourselves that were subconsciously formed when we were too young to realize it was happening. Here are some common limiting beliefs:

- I am not enough.

- I am not worthy.

- I am not smart enough.

- People are selfish.

- There's not enough time.

- Bad things always happen to me.

- There's not enough to go around.

- I have no power to change.

- It's too hard.

We all have limits we have to embrace, but we often put limits on ourselves that prevent us from finding the freedom, peace, and success we desire. We have to be radically honest with ourselves to find that line. If you have fallen into black-and-white thinking or using terms like *always* and *never*, you are likely acting out of fear or a limiting belief. If it is negative or demeaning or rooted in a desire for power or control, it is fear or a limiting belief. If you use the belief as an excuse, it's likely a limiting belief. You will feel it in your body if it isn't true or if it needs to be challenged. It won't feel good and will leave you unsettled, while a true limit is something you would be more open to accept.

Even if your childhood and life have been "normal," the exploration you're doing in this chapter will likely surprise you. Several of my clients say their childhoods were great, but we've found that even then, they still have fears and limiting beliefs driving their thoughts, actions, and choices on a daily basis that were shaped by their early experiences. The focus of this reflection is not to relive difficult experiences in our lives. Instead, it is to uncover those fears and limiting beliefs that are impacting our lives today. We want to find them and understand them so that we can lay them down and let them go. We want to break the patterns that are unknowingly holding us back from living our best life and doing our best work.

As you explore the questions in the Power of Reflection exercise, you may feel angry or ashamed about what comes up. I will keep saying this over and over to you because it's true: this is completely normal. I have been doing this work for myself for years, and I still get stuck thinking from and acting out of these core beliefs that I know are not true. It's important to allow and invite your genuine feelings, then move quickly from anger and shame to curiosity and compassion. Healing is complicated. It's not something that you just get to check off the list and move on from. Be patient with yourself. Give yourself grace. Piling on anger and shame will just make your journey harder, and the journey is difficult enough.

You may also discover feelings of resentment and anger toward others. Letting yourself acknowledge and process those feelings and move toward forgiveness is a key part of this step. It's not something we are often taught how to do because we are encouraged to stuff down, ignore, or avoid our emotions. Try the following exercise and see how you feel.

IDENTIFYING OUR EMOTIONS, THEN PROCESSING AND RELEASING OUR FEELINGS

Emotions create energy, and that energy lives inside us. When something troubling or difficult happens, we feel some way about it first. If we don't know how to identify our emotions and process our feelings, they can overwhelm us and prevent us from taking the next step, or they can stay with us and settle in our body. The situation may be over, but those feelings are still sticking around and piling up. As a result, we can feel anxious and overwhelmed.

The following exercise can help you get free of those feelings and move forward. You can use this exercise for a recent upsetting situation or to go back in time and release feelings associated with past situations that you've been holding on to for a long time.

Get quiet and still. Close your eyes if you can, and settle into your body using your reconnection routine. Recall the situation that upset you and picture yourself in it like you are an observer. Calmly notice and name the emotion you are experiencing. With that emotion in mind, notice how you feel. What physical sensations are you experiencing? Tightness in your chest, nausea, sweaty palms, or heat up your neck might be natural sensations.

Wherever you feel discomfort, acknowledge that this is a feeling that needs to be released for you to heal and move forward. No one is making you feel this way, it's just a sensation. In this current moment, you can choose to release it, and you can shift how you interpret your experience of this situation and respond. You own your experience and your feelings. You can take back your power and free yourself from having to depend on anyone else to feel differently. You have the power to release the emotions, and when you do that, your energy will shift.

Releasing your emotions and shifting your energy could be as simple as breathing. In and out, in and out until you feel the tension release. Other options include big sighs, shouting, singing, dancing, walking, exercising, punching a pillow, whatever might help release that emotion from your body. Try different things until you feel the release. If it doesn't come, go about your day and try this exercise again later.

Remember, you can experience release and even forgiveness without reconciliation or the situation changing. It can actually work in your favor to come to a place of peace before attempting reconciliation. If you have felt some release, check in with yourself. What else do you need? If you would like to speak with

continued

the person involved in your experience from a place of love and respect, then write down what you would like to say and consider having that conversation. If you still feel hurt or angry, keep working at it. Eventually those feelings will be transformed.

Reflect on and celebrate your progress. How did this change you? When we take ownership of our feelings and learn to respond rather than react, we begin to heal, and our healing changes the world around us. This exercise creates more compassion and love for ourselves and others. Reflecting on the impact of this practice and the lessons it taught us encourages us to continue to use it and to share it with others. A wholehearted human being—in their personal life and as a leader—is one who does not project or dump their emotions on others but has a healthy way to process them.

Remember that healing is a long process that takes patience. Each small step makes a difference. It matters. Allow yourself to be uncomfortable. Find support. Document your thoughts and feelings, so you can witness the progress. Positive change will happen if you are committed to doing the work.

REFLECT ON YOUR JOURNEY

- What have you learned, unlearned, or relearned in this chapter?
- What has been most valuable to you?
- What one thing will you commit to doing differently going forward?
- Who can you invite in to keep you accountable?

CHAPTER 3

Identifying Influences

I am broken. I am a burden. These are the secrets I carried around for most of my life.

No one else would tell you that. I didn't show it, but deep down, these were the thoughts that ran my days. Regardless of how good life got, I was convinced something bad was going to happen. No matter what nice things people said about me or did for me, I was terrified they would find out the truth of who I was—unworthy and unlovable. I was constantly working to keep people from seeing the truth, to keep up this facade I had created. Every day, I woke up on the defensive, ready to do whatever it took to maintain my image.

It started when I was little. I believed that I was the reason the people I loved the most fought and that the pain I endured was because of me. Knowing I had this secret, I did everything I could to make people believe that I had a great life and that I was good. I had to have good clothes. My hair had to look good. I had to get good grades. I had to be the best at everything I did.

The trend continued as I went to college, graduated, and got a job. I worked hard to maintain a certain image, letting very few people know or see the real me. I smiled when I wanted to cry. I worked when I wanted to rest. I said yes when I wanted to say no. I went about my day and told my coworkers I was fine just a day after I was in a violent fight with a boyfriend who choked me. I had been living this way for so long that when I said I was OK, I actually started to believe it because it was all I knew. I had accepted that this was just the way it was, and I didn't even realize that I was lying to myself or anyone else.

Subtle messages from family, friends, and teachers had reinforced my belief that I was broken and a burden. I often felt like or even was told I was "difficult" or a "disappointment," when I didn't follow the rules or wanted to do something different, when I didn't get good grades or messed up, when I was sad or angry. Let me be clear: people weren't trying to be mean to me. Often, they didn't even say these words out loud. But I subconsciously sought any message to affirm that narrative. It's what we do, and in doing so, we keep ourselves trapped in our own personal hell. These are the kinds of stories we tell ourselves without necessarily realizing all the places they came from and how we may have added to them ourselves.

TRANSFORMING OUR HEARTS AND MINDS

People who were influential in my life said a lot of nice things about me and to me. They encouraged me and planted seeds for the day I would be willing to let go of the untruths I was telling myself and start to build a new foundation. I couldn't see it at the time, but they were a critical part of helping me on my path of healing and wholeness. Over time, I came to see that I had to do four critical things differently in order to shift the narrative I had long held to the positive and true narrative that was there the whole time:

1. Remember and believe that I am not my thoughts.

2. Identify people I respect and trust, and listen to their voices more than the voices of others.

3. Take in and internalize the positive feedback as much as or more than the negative.

4. Be intentional about what I am filling my head and heart with.

The day I learned that I am not my thoughts changed everything. For my entire life, I had believed that I am who I am. That I was just wired a certain way, and that was that. That I and others would have to deal with it. Then I learned this idea from therapy and other healers that I actually have the ability to witness and control my thoughts as a bystander. My thoughts are not me. They are separate from me. These thoughts of "I am broken" and "I am a burden" are not necessarily true, and I have a choice in whether or not I believe them and act on or react to them. Whoa!

I'll tell you that there was some freedom in this idea, and there was also a great sense of responsibility that I wasn't sure I was willing to take on. I had used these thoughts as excuses my whole life. When I failed, when a relationship didn't work out, when something didn't go my way, I blamed it on those two narratives and let myself wallow in self-pity and victimhood.

For instance, I struggled with romantic relationships through high school, college, and after. I dated several boys and men who were violent and controlling. I blamed it on the fact that I grew up not having the relationship I wanted with my dad and being hurt by him. I blamed him for the mistakes I was making today. I had myself locked in a cycle of despair and destruction. Now I had to choose: I could stay in this comfortable place with these excuses and play the victim, or I could take ownership of my life, my behavior, and my decisions, which meant letting go of excuses and taking full responsibility for my actions. No one else to blame but me. That was scary!

To believe and understand that you are not your thoughts, you need space. Most of us are rushing around, urgently moving from task to task. We don't leave time for awareness, processing, and reflection, which are key to making a positive shift in your thoughts. This is why meditation has become so popular and been so impactful in the lives of many. By quieting everything around us, we create space for awareness. Now, if you are resistant to the idea of meditation, stick with me! This can happen in seconds—you don't need a lot of time right out of the gate.

When you have small moments of silence, bring yourself to the present moment. These happen all the time: waiting in line at the grocery store (stay off your phone), driving the car alone (turn off the radio), maybe even when you're in the bathroom! Take these small moments to check in with yourself. How are you feeling? What are you thinking? Write down what you find and examine it for patterns. Many of my clients are resistant to writing things down because they are fearful that someone might find what they write. I understand this, but it's more impactful to see it down on paper in front of you and easier to recognize patterns. The important thing is that you practice awareness and become familiar with the feelings you are having and the thoughts you are thinking, so you can challenge their validity.

TRANSFORMING YOUR NARRATIVE

Let's create a plan for identifying the stories you are telling yourself so that you can positively transform them. First, consider the following question:

- What are the small moments in your life in which you can start to create awareness of your thoughts and feelings?

What breaks do you have in your day? Before the family gets up. Driving to work. After you park and before you enter the building. When you transition from one task to another. Your lunch break. When you pull in the driveway before you go inside your home. Before you go to bed. These are just a few examples to show that even when you're busy, you do have space for creating more awareness.

Once you have committed to when you will do this, document the following over a week's time:

- How are you feeling in this moment?
- What are you thinking about right now?
- What thoughts, words, or phrases are on your mind?

After your days of reflection, look at what you wrote and see whether there are any commonalities and patterns. Ask yourself:

- Which thoughts do you need to let go of or shift?
- What is one thing you can do to improve the stories you are telling yourself?

GETTING TO THE HEART OF TRANSITION

As you become aware of your answers in doing the Transforming Your Narrative exercise, you should start to see where you might need to do some intentional work to change the natural narrative that has developed in your head. You might not feel ready because maybe you believe some of those negative thoughts. That's OK. I have been there too.

Just a few years ago, I began to realize that one of the underlying narratives that went along with "I am broken" was that I was not worthy of love without condition. Now, I believe in my head that everyone is worthy of love, regardless of their past mistakes, choices, or current behavior. This is something I have come to know as truth through my faith walk, and I can feel it settle into my heart as true. Back then, though, I knew in my head that the thought of "I am not worthy of love without condition" was not true, but I couldn't get there in my heart.

This unhealthy thought was revealed during a healing session, and my teacher asked me to heal this wound by looking at myself in the mirror every day and saying the opposite: "I am worthy of love without condition." Affirmations can be a powerful way of practicing your way into believing and shifting your heart when you know something but have not yet come to believe it.

In my first attempt at doing this self-healing work, I couldn't even get "I am" out without crying. It took me dozens of attempts to say "I am worthy of love without condition" to myself in the mirror before I could get all the words out. It took several dozen more attempts for me to be able to say it out loud without crying, and as I continued to work at it, the belief that the statement was true started to settle into my heart. I finally reached a point where it was my new natural narrative and I was free of that old burden. Sometimes, we are able to heal ourselves if we are willing to acknowledge the truth, beauty, and goodness inside us, accept the Divine Love available to us, and put in the work.

There are other times when we aren't able to get there on our own. We need the support of others inside our story to heal. We need to welcome trusted, loving people into the deepest parts of our hearts and minds, those places we keep hidden. We need community. This takes me to the second critical step in shifting your narrative: identify people you respect and trust, and listen to their voices more than the voices of others.

THE PEOPLE WHO HAVE INFLUENCED WHO WE'VE BECOME

As human beings, we are wired to listen to and believe the negative. It's unfortunate that when we get a negative review or comment, we are more likely to believe it than when someone pays us a compliment. Becoming aware of this is a key part of our healing journey. We also need to consider where those opinions and narratives are coming from. So often in our life, the loudest voices get the most attention, and more often than not, those loud voices are not people we trust, admire, or respect. Realizing this single truth can be very powerful. Why would we listen to people we don't trust, admire, or respect when they share their opinions, especially of us?

Because of our negative experiences with feedback, we stop seeking any feedback from others, and in order for us to create positive shifts in our life, that needs to change. On my own journey, I started to think about who I admired, respected, and trusted. I asked for their advice and opinions. Instead of the judgment I had received before, I started to get positive, respectful feedback about what I did well and what I could do better. Researchers say that you are the sum of the five people you spend the most time with. I know this to be true from my own experience. My life started to drastically change when I was intentional about who I was spending time with and who I sought counsel from.

YOUR INFLUENCES

Take some time to consider who has been and who should be influencing your life.

- Who are the people that speak into your life the most?

continued

Make your list and then ask yourself: Do you trust, admire, and respect them? What are they saying to you? What are they influencing you to believe?

- Who do you trust, admire, and respect?

Name at least five people and then consider the following questions:

- How are they impacting your life?
- What influence do they have on your thoughts and actions?
- If you wished they were more influential in your life, what might that look like and how could you make that happen?

THE THINGS WE ARE EXPOSED TO EVERY DAY

The last thing to keep in mind when it comes to identifying influences in our lives is to become aware of and more intentional about what we take in throughout our day. In my own journey, I started to realize just how much cultural influences had impacted my view of myself and what was meaningful in life. I was taking in negativity all over the place. What I watched, what I listened to on the radio, what I read, what I ate—it was all reinforcing my beliefs that I was broken and a burden, not good enough. I started with small shifts by thinking about what made me feel the best while I was doing it but the worst after, like how a Big Mac tasted so good while I was eating it but made me feel horrible for hours afterward. Like staying out all night only to be exhausted the next day or bingeing Netflix or dessert. Sometimes it's worth it, and sometimes it isn't.

I came to realize there were books and magazines I was reading and music I was listening to that, upon reflection, made me feel worse. The magazines promoted an impossible standard of beauty and advertised all the things I needed to buy to keep up and be somebody. I realized that these magazines actually made me feel worse, encouraged the idea that I wasn't good enough, and weren't teaching me anything worthwhile. The lyrics of the music I listened to were filled with violent and sexual innuendos. These weren't conscious choices I made, and I never thought much of them. Everyone was reading and listening to them, so I thought I should too.

When I was really honest with myself about how I felt after listening to one of those songs, I couldn't deny the yucky feelings in my body. As a society and culture, we are so regularly confronted with violence and sexuality that our tolerance for them is very high. We don't even realize they're impacting us because they're all we've ever known. As I eliminated those magazines and that music from my life, I gained more and more freedom from the thoughts and behaviors they were reinforcing. I desired fewer material things. I found beauty in all forms. I appreciated my own body and looks for what they were. I became less jealous. My temper wasn't so short. On and on.

We can make some profoundly positive changes if we are willing to confront the realities of what we consume and choose differently. There are a couple of things to keep in mind as we do this. First, you can feel shame and guilt as you grow your awareness around what you've been consuming. Do your best to drop those feelings. What's done is done, and you have a chance to start new from here. Don't allow your energy to keep you stuck in the past. Instead, use that energy to propel you into a better future. Second, take it slow. As with anything, I always encourage my clients to keep change simple and choose consistency over intensity. Eliminate or change one thing at a time for a period, so it becomes integrated and you are aware of the ways in which you feel better. Allow it to stick and then choose one more thing to let go of or add in.

If the exercises in this chapter have been challenging for you then congratulations! You have done the hard work in the first two chapters and have the courage to be open and honest with yourself. No matter what our life experiences are, we all have challenging stories we tell ourselves. Just as we peel back one layer, we find another. Do not let this be discouraging. With each layer comes more freedom and compassion for yourself and for others.

By answering the questions in this chapter, you are working the muscles it takes to be resilient and to live a full life. You will consistently face challenges, but when you are equipped with the understanding and the tools to take control of your thoughts and positively shape and influence them, things will get easier and more enjoyable. There will be no more pressure to hide or defend. You can simply be yourself and show up more fully as who you are. After all, that's the goal, isn't it?

REFLECT ON YOUR JOURNEY

- What have you learned, unlearned, or relearned in this chapter?

- What has been most valuable to you?

- What one thing will you commit to doing differently going forward?

- Who can you invite in to keep you accountable?

CHAPTER 4

Discovering Patterns

Before we dive into this chapter, review what you have explored and discovered so far in Chapters 1–3. What insights have you found? What have you learned about yourself? The journey of living with intention and leading with meaning requires us to reflect in order to identify trends and patterns that have been formed out of our beliefs. Much of what we think and do are the result of patterns we are completely unaware of. This practice of reflection allows us to become aware of things we never noticed before as we live day to day. When we pull back and take a look at the bigger picture and broaden our perspective, we can see things in a new way and become more mindful and intentional versus falling into patterns that have a negative impact on us or hold us back.

PATTERNS IN OUR THINKING

As we move through our life experiences, we start to make assumptions about certain things that help us make decisions faster and more effectively.

The trouble is that as we get older and our circumstances change, some of those old patterns of thinking can actually hold us back, and some of those assumptions are no longer valid. For instance, when we're young and naïve, we are taught that strangers are dangerous. In having a natural curiosity and without the ability to discern, we might get into a car with someone who wants to harm us. However, if we don't evolve that pattern of thought—that strangers are dangerous—as we get older, we will miss opportunities to form and grow relationships that could be keys to living a healthy life or having a successful career.

There are so many examples of patterns of thinking that can keep us stuck and should be examined and challenged. My clients have uncovered all sorts of patterns and assumptions, including:

- People can't change.

- Relationships should be easy.

- Money will solve my problems.

- Someday, I will have everything figured out.

- I must do everything I can to make others happy.

Some of these patterns are rooted in black/white, either/or thinking. Looking at the world in this way can be advantageous when it comes to the speed of decision-making and preventing overwhelm, but it is also a disadvantage to our long-term growth. This type of thinking limits our impact, keeps us and our thinking small, and causes us to miss opportunities to learn and grow.

Some of our common patterns are rooted in a desire for comfort. Safety is a deep motivator. It sits near the base of Maslow's hierarchy of needs, a model that psychologist Abraham Maslow created to help us understand the various motivations and needs that drive human behavior. (Physiological needs—such as breathing, food, water, shelter, sleep—are at the bottom of the hierarchy, and safety and security are on the next level.) The danger is found in how our desire for safety can grow into a desire for comfort. Once we feel safe, we start to build our lives around what makes us most comfortable. We avoid challenging situations, difficult conversations, and hard truths. Pursuing comfort will leave you frustrated or worse yet, stuck. If you want to grow, you can't be comfortable. If you want to be in healthy relationships with others, you won't be comfortable. You might have a lot in common with someone, yet you are still different. It takes consistent effort and work to grow and to build good relationships in life, work, and community.

Some of our common patterns are rooted in attachment. We want things. We believe that once we get certain things or reach a certain place, we will be content, satisfied, or happy. Wanting things is not bad, but attaching our feelings to them is. When we tie our emotions to things, we create opportunities to be frustrated and disappointed. A healthier perspective is to choose to be content, satisfied, and happy now and stay in pursuit of what we want.

Other common patterns are rooted in control. We don't like to admit it, but if we are honest with ourselves, we aren't in control of much. We put a lot of effort into trying to control others or external circumstances that we can't. People pleasers, pay attention: You cannot control how other people feel. You can exhaust yourself and deplete all your energy trying to control the emotions of someone else and most of the time, you will be left feeling depleted and resentful because the fact is, you cannot control how others feel. If I could free people of one thing, it would be this. Be thoughtful. Be kind. Let go of the rest.

For achievers, there is another issue around control. You get wrecked when something ruins what you thought would be, or you get stuck in what you hoped for instead of moving into what is or what could be. It's good to have dreams and goals and plans, but you also need to put some effort into letting them go. If you can refocus on becoming intentional about where you spend your time, energy, and resources—if you can be diligent about your inputs and allow for pivots based on the realities of life—then you can accept the outcomes. This letting go has to happen to live in this reality. You have to be willing to acknowledge things as they are, focus on what you can control, and move your energy from resistance to acceptance.

WHAT THOUGHT PATTERNS KEEP SHOWING UP IN YOUR LIFE?

Let's explore your patterns. Think about recurring themes, situations, or other feelings that pop up in your life that don't feel good. Evaluate the list of assumptions earlier in this chapter for ideas to get you started. Once you have your list, consider where these patterns may have come from. As humans, it brings us peace to know why. You may be able to find that answer based on your life experience, and you may not. If you can't pinpoint original events or roots, don't stay stuck in those questions. That's not the important part of this exercise. We can break old patterns without understanding where they came from or why they formed.

Make a list of your recurring themes and assumptions and then ask yourself:

- Where did these originate or what are they rooted in?
- What do these thoughts say about you?
- How do these thought patterns impact your view of yourself, others, and the world?

PATTERNS IN OUR BEHAVIOR

I have a pattern of rescuing that started early in my life. When things got intense at home, I became the person in our family who was trying to make sure everyone was OK and fix it. That continued into my friend groups and day-to-day relationships. It even carried into my work. As I was elevated to a leadership position, I started taking on more and more as my team members came to me with issues. I would jump in to fix them instead of creating space for them to learn themselves. I created dependencies on me in small ways, and then I became stressed out and resentful they couldn't solve their own issues—and in my view, I was the only one with the power to fix it.

It started innocently enough. Someone would ask a question, and instead of challenging them to think it through and putting the issue back in their hands, I would simply provide the answer. This created a pattern by which all decisions were funneled to and through me. As the team grew, the number of issues grew, and you can imagine how squeezed I felt being the bottleneck for every issue that popped up! To break this pattern, I have had to do two very practical things:

1. Pause and breathe. When someone comes to me with a question or an issue, I imagine it as a beach ball between us. I ask myself who is best to solve this issue and who is responsible for solving it? What is my role in this? If it is their issue to solve and they hand it to me, then my job is to put it back in their hands and provide the coaching, support, and questions for them to solve it, so they can go back into the game and carry it with confidence. Taking that little time out prevents me from jumping in to fix it.

2. Take inventory and delegate. Because I am not perfect at the pause and breathe practice, I continue to pick up balls that are

not mine. On a weekly basis, and at high volume times on a daily basis, I have to sit with my list of to-dos and take inventory of my thoughts and feelings to check in with myself about what's mine and what needs to be delegated. (You can use the dumping exercise from Chapter 1 for this.)

As a rescuer, I create dependencies where there shouldn't be any, and when I feel the weight of people needing me getting heavier, I panic. I want to be wanted, not needed, but my old patterns and habits have to continue to shift, and that is my work to do. As I continue to work through this, it feels very selfish. I am staying out of things I used to get involved in. I am saying no where I used to say yes. I am no longer living out what people expect of me, which can make them confused, frustrated, and sometimes upset. A shift in relationships is to be expected when we break old patterns that are no longer serving us. Over the long term, it's a good thing. The challenge is to stick it out and work through it together with those you have and want to keep relationships with, until, ideally, you are both shifted into a new and healthier pattern. This takes time and requires both parties to participate and adjust. Sometimes you have to do your part and wait for the other person to come along. You can't force them into a new pattern; they have to find their way alongside you. Do your part and all that you can, and allow them to do theirs.

Let's explore common patterns of behavior without judgment, because we all fall into them, and we will forever be a work in progress. There are expansive patterns that open and elevate us and constrictive patterns that hold us back. Here we are identifying constrictive patterns, the ones that we might not be aware of that prevent us from reaching our potential. Here are some examples:

- Blaming
- Playing victim
- Catastrophizing (consistently playing out the worst-case scenario)
- Ruminating (staying stuck on something)
- Deflecting responsibility
- Rescuing
- Protecting
- Being a people pleaser
- Appeasing

It can be helpful to use specific scenarios when you start identifying these patterns. Think about times in your life when you felt frustrated, hurt, or resentful. Are there common patterns there? Placing blame and playing victim are constrictive patterns we all fall into. It is difficult to take full responsibility for our lives, but these patterns give our power away. We can't learn and change if we are always blaming and playing victim. Yes, people will hurt us. Taking responsibility for our part in it does not excuse their actions; it simply gives us the power to move forward in a better way.

I could blame a lot of my own issues, patterns, and habits on the abuse that I suffered at the hands of others throughout my life. I spent the first quarter of my life doing that, and it kept me stuck. I was living in the past and using the phrase "if only . . ." a lot. I was so focused on what was that I had no room to consider what could be. Reaching your potential requires the courage to let go of what was, to face the reality of what is, and to take responsibility for what will be. Are you brave enough to make those shifts in your life, leadership, and work?

WHAT BEHAVIORAL PATTERNS
KEEP SHOWING UP IN YOUR LIFE?

Let's consider the behaviors that go along with the patterns you uncovered and what perception that creates about you. For some patterns, your behaviors will create a perception opposite of what you want people to think about you. For instance, if you want to be perceived as a strong and responsible leader, then playing victim is a pattern you want to break. For other patterns, the behaviors might present a favorable perception of you that will make it harder to shift the pattern. In my example of rescuing, I was perceived as helpful. To break the pattern, I had to deal with being perceived as "pushing back" or even being selfish or unhelpful. I had to take the long-term view and show my teammates that I wanted to empower them, not enable them, so that we could all learn and grow in a sustainable and healthy way. Your turn.

Make a list of behavioral patterns you've observed and consider these questions:

- Where did these originate or what are they rooted in?
- What do these behaviors say about you?
- How do these behavioral patterns impact your view of yourself, others, and the world?

Consider one pattern you'd like to break or shift. What is one simple thing you can do differently when you find yourself in that pattern? Sometimes, it's simply pausing and breathing so you can become aware that you are in that pattern. That is a first step, even if you continue to carry out the pattern. Become aware and then add one more thing you can do to shift in a positive way.

Think about who can help you in this process. Tell a trusted friend, colleague, or significant other about what you've discovered and what you'd like to do differently. They can be your

accountability buddy in helping you continue to create awareness of the pattern and making shifts. Baby steps matter. Take it
slow and be gentle with yourself. These patterns are likely deeply
ingrained, and it will take work and a lot of repetition to shift
them. Keep trying! Make more space for silence, stillness, and
reflection. Running through the scenarios of your day will help
you continue to identify areas you can work on. You can do it!

PATTERNS IN OUR HABITS

Routines and habits make our lives easier. Left unexamined, they can
hold us back from reaching our potential. I had a habit of eating a
store-bought brownie every day at lunch in high school. I didn't think
anything of it until someone educated me on the ill effects of sugary,
processed foods. Then I started to become aware of how I felt after I
ate the brownie and realized that it likely wasn't the best choice for my
health and personal goals.

Growing up, my family got into the routine of going to the mall on
the weekends. Shopping was a leisure activity I had always known. As
I got older, I realized I could make a thousand other choices of what
to do with my time and save a lot of money by shifting that routine.
Buying things wasn't my priority. In fact, I didn't really enjoy the activity of shopping; it was just something I had fallen into and kept doing.

A few years back, my mentor asked me to outline my top priorities.
I named my family as a top priority. He asked me how much of my
time and energy I was dedicating to family. I realized I wasn't focused
on spending time with family or necessarily even making plans with
family, they just got whatever time was left after I fit everything else in.
That was a big wake-up call for me about my habits. Our habits should
reflect our priorities—who we want to be, how we want to serve, who

we want to love. The sad truth is that because of our habits, many of our priorities get assigned the leftovers.

Today, I am actively examining and working on the habit I have around filling my calendar to the point of exhaustion. I cannot remember where this habit originated, but I recall that from a young age, I was encouraged to work hard and was complimented on my work ethic. Along the way, I became afraid of being called lazy. I enjoyed being recognized for what I accomplished—honestly, I still do. I think that helped form my addiction to productivity and getting things done. What that says about me that I know is unhealthy is that I don't believe I am good enough or worthy of love just for *being*—without any of the *doing* to earn that. It also signals to my family that they aren't as important as my work because I have nothing left in the tank to give them when I get home.

To shift this habit, I have been working to consider how I contribute to the world by my *being*, and I have been keeping (holding close and top of mind) the accolades I receive from others that have more to do with who I am than what I have done. I am also reflecting on the quality of time I spend with family and friends and on how I feel physically, emotionally, mentally, and spiritually, so I can keep my *doing* in check. I believe these practices will help me make a positive shift. Now that you have some examples in mind, let's look at your own habits.

WHAT HABIT PATTERNS
KEEP SHOWING UP IN YOUR LIFE?

Make a list of your habits and consider the following:

- Where did these originate or what are they rooted in?
- What do these habits say about you?
- How do these habit patterns impact your view of yourself, others, and the world?

PATTERNS IN OUR ROUTINES

The most impactful routines are those that happen as soon as we open our eyes for a new day and right before we close them at the end of one. How you begin your day can positively or negatively affect the rest of it, and how you end your day can positively or negatively affect your sleep.

Many of us start our day by checking social media or watching the news. It's what we do because it's what we've seen others do or what is at our fingertips. When we grow up with parents who religiously watch the news each morning, we are likely to do that too because it's all we know. When we have access to our phone because we use it as our alarm clock, it's easy to fall into a routine of checking all of our applications and scrolling first thing in the morning.

I challenge you to consider whether these things make you feel safe and secure and provide a grounded and positive outlook on your day. The news and social media do not represent the whole picture or even the reality of the world we are living in. We see things we cannot control. We witness suffering and other situations that do not represent what's happening where we work and live. We are exposed to the highlight reels of others while sitting in the reality of our life. It is important to be informed, but we have a choice of when we choose to consume this information. Upon waking up, we are trying to find our footing. Don't you want to build your day on a more solid and true foundation than the negative events of the day or someone else's highlight reel?

YOUR MORNING ROUTINE

Take a moment to evaluate your current morning routine and its impact on your well-being. Answer the following questions as honestly as you can:

continued

- What's the first thing you do when you wake up in the morning?
- How does this make you feel?
- How does this impact your thoughts and mood for the day?
- What other routines do you notice about your morning?

After reviewing what you wrote, consider what improvements you can make. Start by envisioning your ideal morning routine and then pick out elements you can start to incorporate into your current routine.

- What would your ideal morning look and feel like?
- What are the most important and impactful elements in that ideal morning?
- If you could only include one element from that morning routine, what would it be?
- How can you incorporate that into your routine starting tomorrow?

Remember, this is all about consistency versus intensity. Small changes matter. You don't want to overhaul your entire routine or make it overly complicated. You also want to be reasonable and realistic about what's possible. Kids, commitments, and other responsibilities put real limits on what our mornings can look like. Accept that reality and do what you can. Most importantly, remember to sit with yourself and reflect on how you feel after you've incorporated new elements, so you become aware of their impact. This will help you stay committed.

The end of your day is another great opportunity to create a routine that can positively impact your life, leadership, and work. On a typical day, we may mindlessly crank up the radio on our evening commute, come home to rush through dinner, so we can watch whatever TV show or read whatever book is popular at the time, and then scroll through our social media feeds until we go to bed. We hear every day that more and more people suffer from anxiety and depression. We do what we can to get through the day, come home exhausted, and do whatever we can to numb out or make ourselves feel better.

What we don't realize is that most of our coping mechanisms leave us feeling even more drained and anxious. Those feelings of anxiety and frustration from the day never get dealt with. They just get shoved aside or deep within us, and the weight of it all continues to build. Our temporary escape is just that—temporary. Is your evening routine serving you and the relationships that are most important to you?

YOUR EVENING ROUTINE

As you did with your morning routine, evaluate your current evening routine and write down your answers:

- What does your typical evening look like?
- How do you feel in the evenings?
- What's the last thing you do before you go to bed?
- How might all of this be impacting your relationships? Your goals? Your overall sense of peace? Your sleep?
- Considering what you just wrote, think about your ideal evening routine:
- What would your ideal evening routine look and feel like?
- What are the most important and impactful elements in that ideal evening?
- If you could only include one element from that evening routine, what would it be?
- How can you incorporate that into your routine starting tomorrow?

If it's been difficult to envision your ideal morning and evening routines, consider making a list of people you admire, and find out what their morning and evening routines look like. We are all different and have different priorities, so there is no one-size-fits-all approach. That's why it's important to find out what's working for others, explore alternative perspectives, try some, and keep what works.

For example, I know myself well enough to understand that I need spiritual and heart-centered (loving, compassionate narratives and stories) content in the mornings. I am a naturally assertive person who lives in my head, so I choose content in the mornings that will bring me into my heart and soften me up. This helps me be more wholly myself, and it allows me to come into my day feeling my best. When I choose a business podcast or aggressive music, I come into my day too much in my head and with too much aggressive energy. I feel restless and impatient, and my behavior follows suit. As you get more in tune with who you are and why you are the way you are, you will understand what you need. Let it develop over time.

HOW OUR PATTERNS IMPACT US AS LEADERS

So far in our journey, we have mostly explored our personal identities and lives, but there are times throughout the book when I will go into more detail about our identities as leaders and how our vision for who we've become as a leader has been formed. The stories, tools, and lessons I share in each of these sections are designed to help you achieve your full potential in all aspects of your life where you lead. Note that when I speak about leaders, I am not referring to a formal position but to a call that all of us are asked to fulfill in different facets of our lives. We each live in community (connected and interdependent), for example, and so we may be called to be a leader of some group or for some activity.

Let's look at leadership now through the lens of our patterns. We lead with who we are, so to be a good leader, whether in our families, workplaces, or communities, we have to do the deep exploration and healing work to become our best self.

Early in our life we are taught to follow. Most of our educational and societal structures encourage us to follow. The conversation around leadership in this chapter is intended to help you break out of the pattern of following in your heart, mind, and behavior and step into leadership where you are called to lead. But I don't see leadership as something to be held constantly. We lead in situations and relationships when we need to and follow when we need to. The world is calling on leaders to be more open and collaborative—to know when to step up and when to step back.

I regularly see several key patterns with my clients that prevent them from reaching their potential as leaders. Some are habits that were developed from how they worked and how they were celebrated when they were an individual contributor. But our patterns and habits need to change when we move from being an individual contributor to leading a team of people. Some of these habits for leading a team are formed from our exposure to cultural definitions of leadership that are rooted in power and control.

For example, instead of waiting for direction, leaders take the initiative. Instead of bringing problems to the table, leaders bring solutions. Leaders have routines for how they deal with stress, so they can self-regulate and show up healthy and whole. Leaders take time to pull back and think strategically about the business. Leaders develop habits around communication, inviting ideas and asking people for feedback. Leaders invest time in a routine to develop the vision and culture of the organization. Leaders develop habits of recognition, appreciation, and celebration to support their people.

> ## LEADERS YOU ADMIRE
>
> Think about the leaders you most want to emulate. What are a few words or phrases you would use to describe them? Look at those words. Then ask yourself these questions:
>
> - What do people who can live out those words do?
> - What kind of habits and routines do the people you listed have in their life and work?
> - What do you think their thoughts and beliefs are?

When you move from getting things done yourself to getting things done through others, your whole set of habits and routines needs to shift. We don't train new leaders well in this area. You have a new realm of responsibility and authority. What is the purpose of your role? What outcomes are you responsible for? What is the work to be done? How will you measure and track your progress? How will you celebrate success? When will you plan? When it's your responsibility to develop the answers to these questions, you have to create new routines and habits for yourself. You are no longer taking orders and managing tasks. You have to set up systems and processes for planning, budgeting, reviewing, coaching, developing, and problem-solving. These are the top two mistakes I see managers make:

1. They don't shift out of *doing* by delegating what needs to be accomplished.

2. They don't make time for preparing and managing.

Let's explore why these two mistakes are so common and how they manifest.

Placing Productivity over People

When we start our work life, we get accolades and recognition for the work we get done. When we move into leadership, we are not tasked to get the work done ourselves but to ensure the work gets done through others. This requires a whole new set of habits. We must be in communication with our people. We must spend time with our people. We must help our people manage their work and priorities. We have to set aside our own task list for our people.

In a world of work that is the noisiest and busiest that it's ever been, this can be a significant challenge. Small changes in our habits can ensure that we are putting our people over productivity. In doing this, we raise the level of quality in the work and the effectiveness of our teams. We get the right things done at the right time by the right people. Plus, when we are connected and communicating, our team members are more productive and engaged, and the work becomes more enjoyable.

Creating *containers* for interactions with your team members and scheduling them can help you form better habits. When one of my teammates moved to another city, I scheduled a ten-minute window on my calendar twice per week that worked for her schedule with the intention to simply check in and catch up. We could no longer swing our chairs around and chat or go to lunch together, and we agreed that it was important to maintain our connection in this way. It also helped her feel more connected to the team while she was no longer physically with us and gave us intentional time to build our relationship.

Another small habit that can change things for the better is to set up recurring one-on-one meetings with all of your people. Even when you are with your staff each day, you don't get a full picture of what's happening with a person unless you have uninterrupted and focused time with them. Having a standard set of questions or items to cover can be helpful for these conversations. These can be something as simple as asking what's going well and what's challenging right now. This allows both of you to come prepared.

I find a one-on-one format that is personal and professional to be helpful. Our team uses the following format, which provides room for the person to share how they're doing as a human. It starts us off with positivity, helps us stay on track with commitments from the last meeting, empowers the person to understand and update on their goals, provides space for questions and concerns, helps them develop action items and focus, and allows for two-way feedback.

- Personal check-in
- Celebrations and recognition
- Updates from last meeting
- Updates on strategic initiatives and individual goals
- Questions, concerns, and assistance needed
- Focus and priorities between now and the next meeting
- Team/organizational updates
- Feedback

Research shows that investing as little as one hour per month in a one-on-one format can significantly improve engagement, morale, connection, and trust. In our work, we have found the most connected, engaged, and effective teams have leaders that meet with team members one-on-one every other week. The preceding format requires an hour, but if that seems like more time than you can afford or not as much is changing in your environment, consider how you could break up the agenda and format or find a cadence that works best for your team members. The point is to create connection, improve communication, and allow your team members to be seen, heard, and appreciated. Remember: if you schedule it, honor it. I see many leaders put one-on-ones on the calendar but then cancel them or keep pushing them back because they are "too busy" with other things. This sends a strong message to your team that they are not important.

Telling and Talking versus Asking and Listening

When I moved into a leadership position, I instantly felt the pressure to have all the answers. This misperception about leadership can cause a lot of undue stress on teams. As the leader, we feel pressure to have the answers and, as a team member, we expect our leader to have the answers. The leader starts telling and talking, leaving the team members frustrated because they don't feel seen or heard, and most of what the leader says doesn't make sense because she doesn't understand the context and consequences like the team does.

What if we flipped those expectations on their head? What if, instead of assuming anything, we listen to each other? And what if, before making any decisions, we work to understand what's happening? What if we admit what we don't know and empower ourselves and our team members to work together to find solutions? In a world that is constantly changing, this is a much better approach. The best leaders in our current environment are those who value listening, understanding, critical thinking, and collaboration. We all have answers, but the best leaders are those willing to put in the work to find the best answers.

Understanding the decision-making process can help us break bad habits, like making assumptions or making statements when we should be asking questions. In any decision, there are three phases that should be worked through:

- Preparing for the decision

- Making the decision
- Executing the decision

Most of us skip phase one and miss a big opportunity to make a more informed and well-rounded decision by including our team, so we have greater buy-in. Instead of going into a meeting with our own assumptions and making decisions based on those, we should pull back and ask questions, include other people, and make sure we have all the information we need to move forward.

Reacting to Requests Instead of Planning for Priorities

When we begin our work journey, someone is dictating to us what should be done by when. As we move into leadership, it can be left unsaid and even forgotten that it is now our responsibility to determine priorities. We must take ownership of this process and determine how to put first things first according to the outcomes we are responsible for. If we don't, there are plenty of people who will ask us to do things that will lead us away from being successful in our role.

A couple of components are key to making this shift: First, we must determine what outcomes we are responsible for and what our level of authority is, then we need to make time and space for preparation and planning. When we accept a new position, we get our title and a general idea of what we are responsible for, but a lot of assumptions are made. Sit down with your boss and really talk through expectations and outcomes.

Once you are clear about the specifics around your responsibilities, authority, expectations, and outcomes, consider what activities will help you live out your vision of success according to those parameters. To do this, ask yourself the following questions and write down your answers:

- Who do I need to be in communication with?

- What relationships matter most?

- What conversations do I need to be having?

- What information do I need to be looking at regularly?

- Who will help me carry out my duties?

- How will I evaluate and communicate progress?

Once you have these items written out, rank them in order of which are most important and then determine how you can rearrange your schedule, so your time and energy are where they need to be. One of the greatest changes we can make to move from reactive to proactive is to start our day with time to plan and prepare, and end our day with reflection and learning. Taking even five minutes in the morning to consider what the two or three most important tasks for the day are and scheduling them into your calendar can help you start to make positive shifts. At the end of the day, reflect on whether you made those things a priority and what you learned.

As you continue this practice, you will see the power of planning, and it will naturally start to expand. If you hold yourself accountable by making time to reflect and learn at the end of the day, you'll start to see what might be getting in the way of putting first things first. Sometimes, priorities need to change, and acknowledging that you are being intentional about shifting priorities is important. Dealing with interruptions and things that come up can be some of the most important and impactful work we do. It can also become an excuse not to do the never urgent but very important things.

As you build this prioritization muscle, you'll find yourself bringing it into your moment-by-moment decision-making by asking yourself the following when something comes up:

- Am I the only one who can do this?
- Do I need to do this now?
- What are the trade-offs if I commit to this?

These and other important questions will become your norm and ensure you get better and better at putting the first things first.

Abdicating Responsibility

When we don't have the desire or discipline to do our best and do what's right for the greater good, we can fall into blaming and excuse-making. This is a sad and serious issue in today's world of work and leadership. If I could support a positive change in leadership patterns across the world, I would pick this category because I believe it would have the deepest and most sustainable impact on our society.

I cannot tell you how many times we come into environments where the executives blame the managers and frontline staff and vice versa. Sometimes we have to listen hard for it because it is disguised as the executives investing in team members to "help them level up," and in that sentiment, we can hear and see an unwillingness to consider that the executive team might have some responsibility to change as well. When things aren't going as well as we'd hoped, it can quickly turn into an us-versus-them game covered up in nice language.

When there are issues inside our organizations or teams, these are the first questions we should ask ourselves:

- What part of this could be me?
- What might I not know or see?
- How might others be viewing this another way?

These and other questions that point us back to ourselves take courage and humility to ask, and those characteristics are exactly what we need. It's easy to focus on what everyone else needs to do or should change, but the greatest test of leadership is the willingness to ask ourselves what we need to do or change.

When things aren't going as we'd hoped, we don't always have the ability to influence or change the direction, system, or process. In these situations, we are challenged to change what we can control: our thoughts, words, and actions. And when things still don't feel right and we have a choice, we can choose to take a risk and change our circumstances.

Assessing and Evolving Your Leadership Patterns

My first job out of college was better than I ever could have dreamed of. I had my heart set on working in the nonprofit sector in a service-oriented organization, but my professor kindly reminded me of the student loans I'd racked up and encouraged me to find a for-profit company with a good culture, so I could start paying off my loans and pursue my passion later.

I accepted a marketing job in a sector of business I was unfamiliar with. I have to say I wasn't thrilled about the job itself, but it was a great company, with great people, great learning and development, and great opportunities for advancement, and I had a great leader who was eager to help me grow. Instead of coming into that job thinking about it as something I was doing to pay off my loans and just get by until I could do what I really wanted to do, I decided I wanted to do my best and learn everything I could. On my career journey, this was shift number one.

A couple of years into my role, I got bored. It wasn't that I didn't like the work, but I was no longer challenged by it. Instead of putting myself in coast-mode or blaming my boss for not giving me more challenging assignments, I let him know how I felt and asked him what options I could explore. We evaluated opportunities to grow in my role and looked at other roles, and eventually I moved on to something new within the company. This was shift number two.

Toward the end of my time with the company, I had helped build a team from the ground up that I was really proud to be a part of—so proud that I brought work home with me every night, took it personally when others didn't follow through on their commitments, and stressed myself out to the point that I was having health issues. I worked and worked to make shifts in my thoughts, words, and actions. But ultimately, I realized that I was so tied into this role and the team in an unhealthy way that I would have to move on. Someone else could come in and serve in a better way than I could, and I would need to find something new where I could start fresh and reset my boundaries and expectations in a healthier way. This was shift number three.

I have not done all of this perfectly, and I find myself blaming or making excuses to this day, but I'm getting better at not doing this, and it is no longer a habit. These shifts are possible, and they are empowering. Abdicating your responsibility in leadership is detrimental to your growth, to your relationships, to the organization, and ultimately to the world.

WHAT DO OUR PATTERNS SAY ABOUT US?

Discovering our patterns gives us the ability to create positive change. Without awareness of what our patterns are, we continue to react our way through life and give our power away. It's worth slowing down to examine your life, so you can live, lead, and work more intentionally. Nothing has to change for everything to change. Even if your external circumstances stay the same, an internal transformation can drastically change how you think and feel—and eventually change everything.

FINAL REVIEW OF YOUR PATTERNS

Let's do a final review of all the patterns you have discovered. Consider the following questions:

- What false narratives or limiting beliefs have been built out of your patterns?
- What do these patterns say to the world about who you are?
- What impacts have your patterns had on you? On your relationships? On your work? In your leadership?
- What pattern is your first priority to change in a positive way?

Be patient with yourself in this process and continue to revisit these questions from time to time. As we have new life and leadership experiences, new patterns develop. This is a continuous and ongoing process. There is no shame in realizing that some of our patterns have not been good for us. Remember, when we know better, we can do better, and that's all we can do. We are a constant work in progress, and we are always evolving. Making these shifts can be challenging and will require patience. Awareness is the first step.

REFLECT ON YOUR JOURNEY

- What have you learned, unlearned, or relearned in this chapter?
- What has been most valuable to you?
- What one thing will you commit to doing differently going forward?
- Who can you invite in to keep you accountable?

CHAPTER 5

Inviting Perspective

Before you take action on what you learned about your patterns in the last chapter, let's explore deeper by inviting in the perspective of others. You may think you're on the right track, but inviting trusted allies and confidants into your journey may reveal a whole new way of thinking and a new set of things to consider.

THE SIGNIFICANCE OF FEEDBACK

How does feedback make you feel? Positive feedback makes me feel embarrassed, and critical feedback makes me feel defensive, but I have forced myself to push past those feelings because inviting the perspective of others has been a key part of my growth and development. We don't reach our full potential on our own. We need others speaking into us and providing us with their perspective and challenging our own, and we should welcome it.

There are a few things to keep in mind before you rush out to get feedback. First, where are you on the scale of critical to confident? If you are someone who is constantly criticizing yourself and focused on everything you are doing wrong, start by seeking perspectives about your gifts and what you are doing right. If you are someone who is confident and you consistently get praise and feel solid about where you are in life, leadership, and work, you may need to seek feedback that challenges you.

Second, who do you respect, and who cares about you? When seeking feedback, the source is important. You need to go to people you admire and respect—people who share the same values and who you want to be like. If you can find someone you respect who holds different viewpoints and has a different perspective and experience than you, even better. You also need to be sure those people really care about you. Giving critical or challenging feedback can be difficult, and only those who really care will take the time to be honest with you.

Third, allow time to contemplate the feedback and remember that this is simply someone's perspective; it is not necessarily the truth and typically does not represent the full picture. We are not great at objectively judging ourselves or others. This is why some leaders and organizations have done away with the rating and review processes in the workplace altogether. The danger in not inviting in other perspectives at all is that you won't get the information you need to understand how you are perceived by others. Most of what we do involves other people, and if we don't understand how we are impacting the people around us, how will we improve our ability to be in relationships with others, be part of a community, and grow our influence and leadership?

TIPS FOR GATHERING FEEDBACK

When requesting feedback, it's important to ask for specifics and provide context about why and what you are seeking. If you have certain aspects of your life and work you want to improve, share them. Also share why you are reaching out and why you have chosen this individual to speak into your life. If you can't identify specifics, simply let the person know that you trust, admire, and respect them and you are looking for ways to proactively improve your life, work, and leadership. If you can't come up with specific questions, using the start, stop, and continue method can be powerful:

- Start—What do I need to start doing?

- Stop—What do I need to stop doing?

- Continue—What do I need to continue doing?

This gives people a basic framework for providing specific and actionable feedback versus a broad question like "What could I do better?"

As you seek out feedback, keep in mind that you will start to hear things that may be difficult or challenging to your ego. People who care about us the most are not only willing to encourage us, they are willing to challenge us to become our best self. While it doesn't always feel like it at the moment, this is a true gift. It's OK that you get defensive; I do too. Breathe through it, give yourself space as needed, and when you're ready, go back and thank that person for loving you enough to be honest about their perspective.

Remember, it is just their perspective and only one piece of the whole of what the person has shared with you. What part of it is true? Sometimes, the other person's perspective is just that . . . perspective. Be honest with yourself about whether there is something useful and true in it for you. Also keep in mind that if you have chosen well, this person has likely provided many words of encouragement and positive feedback before sharing the challenging bit. It's our nature to focus on the negative, but it's most helpful when we can zoom out to look holistically at what they have shared with us.

For most of us, receiving any type of feedback can be challenging. Many of us would almost prefer to hear critical feedback face-to-face than positive feedback because we don't know how to accept the compliments; we dismiss or excuse them. This behavior is destructive to our growth, but it is something we are conditioned to do. "Don't be too confident." "Don't get cocky." "Stay humble." Many of my clients resist positive feedback and affirmations because they are fearful of slipping into the selfish, cocky state they have been warned about or despise in others. Trust yourself. You know where that line is. We all walk it, and we all cross it from time to time. I'd rather you cross it every once in a while than hold yourself back from receiving at all.

If we block ourselves from receiving, we cut off what is life-giving for us—positive words and affirmations can be the fuel that can keep us going. This is especially detrimental to someone like me who felt like they were a burden or broken. I put myself in a perpetual give-and-fix mode. I had broken the natural cycle of giving and receiving. This left me depleted, anxious, and resentful. I was so focused on everyone else that I didn't make time to focus on myself in a positive way—to care for, nurture, and love my own self and soul. I also wasn't asking for positive feedback or when I received it, allowing it to settle in and integrate. I was keeping myself from being healthy and whole. When we allow ourselves to receive a positive compliment or affirmation, it heals a part of us and fills us up so we can continue to serve others.

REQUESTING FEEDBACK

Now that you're prepared to gather feedback, let's talk about good questions to ask and who you should receive it from. First, think about which people you would like to have more influence in your life. I suggest going back to your list in Chapter 3 of the people you trust, respect, and admire most to make this new list. Or are there others you could consider? When you have your list of five to seven people ready, you can move on to the following exercise.

REQUESTING FEEDBACK FROM OTHERS

The most powerful questions to ask are broad, open-ended ones that seek someone's perspective of you. These force people to think harder and don't direct them down a certain path or to a particular answer. The data that comes from these types of questions can be full of valuable insights and opportunities to learn. Here are a few questions to consider asking the people on your list:

- Based on what you know about me, what do I do well?
- In your opinion, what could I do better?
- If you choose three words to describe me, what would they be and why?
- From your perspective, what are my unique abilities?
- What things am I not so good at and should leave to someone else or ask for help with?
- What values do you see me display in my everyday life?
- In your experience, what does my life and leadership indicate is meaningful and valuable to me?
- Based on what I say and how I act, what tagline or mantra would you assign to me?

As you start to receive the feedback, hold it out in front of you. How does it make you feel? Why is that? Does it validate something you know or desire to be true about you? Does it conflict with your self-image? Which parts are easy to accept? Which parts are difficult to accept? Sometimes the feedback we get that makes us uncomfortable is exactly what we know

continued

to be true in our hearts but are not ready to reconcile in our minds, and sometimes it is simply another person's insecurities or misperceptions showing through. Only you have the ability to determine the difference through deep reflection, contemplation, and further conversation. Ask for more information or context as needed.

FINDING YOUR LESSONS WITHIN THE OPINIONS OF OTHERS

When I was promoted to my first leadership position, the company I worked for did 360 reviews. For those unfamiliar with this process, a 360 review is a set of questions you ask a number of different people you work with (direct reports, leaders, peers, and others) so they can offer you feedback. There are various formats of questions, rating scales, etc., but the goal is to gather feedback on how others perceive you, what they think you do well, and how they believe you can improve. Per my employer's process, I was asked to invite several people to participate: all my direct reports, the people I reported to, peers I worked with frequently, and anyone else in the organization who had a good line of sight to our leadership and might have valuable input to provide. I think I sent my review request to more than thirty people, most of whom I interacted with on a daily basis in some way.

When I received the results back, I was given a week or so to read and process them before I met with someone from human resources and my leaders. As I read through the results, most of the marks were good. But there were two things that surprised me and, I'll admit, made me upset. First, many people considered me to be closed-minded, and second, people labeled me as aggressive. As I read those words, I could feel my neck and face growing hotter and a burn deep in my belly. The rage was building. I stewed on those two comments all night that night.

The next day, I decided I needed to talk to someone about it. I couldn't wait a full week until the review with my leader and human resources to defend myself. I socialized my findings to a few of my close friends and trusted team members. Most of them defended me, saying they would never use those words to describe me, the people who shared that feedback must be intimidated by me, and if I were a man, my actions wouldn't be viewed that way. I was building my confidence and my defense.

Then someone I care about and respect shared this simple truth: Even if only one person had that feedback, it was their perception, and their perception was their reality. What part of that feedback could be true? The way she framed this stopped me in my tracks. I was trying to defend my character and integrity. She was telling me there was no way someone could judge my character and integrity because they didn't have the whole story. They were simply sharing their perception of my actions and how I made them feel. No one was saying I *was* closed-minded or aggressive; they were saying they *perceived* me as closed-minded and aggressive. This small way of depersonalizing the issue helped me drop my defenses and be able to look openly and honestly at myself to see what part of my behavior I had an opportunity to improve. What a gift!

I could have written all of the feedback off and continued doing exactly what I was doing. But in setting aside my ego and exploring these comments more deeply, I learned a few things about my approach:

- When I already had my mind made up, I used my responses to convince someone of my way. I didn't really listen to and explore their ideas or what they had to say.

- I didn't establish "safe ground" as my leader called it, when entering a conversation or conflict with someone. My confidence was already intimidating, so this approach would often cause people to completely shut down. For instance, if someone shared an idea, instead of saying something like, "I really like where you're going, what if we also considered . . .," I would simply say something like, "I think we should . . ."

- When I was busy and moving from task to task to get things done, I ran over people. I didn't smile, I brought fierce energy, and I made commands instead of requests.

I could go on, but you get the picture. Now I will say that for a time after this review, I spent a lot of energy working on how I said things—so much energy, in fact, that I started not standing up for ideas at all because I was exhausted by the processes of working so hard not to offend anyone. I lost my sparkle and passion. In working with my own coach, I realized I got to decide what incorporating this feedback and changing my approach looked like for me, and what consequences I was willing to deal with.

To this day, I still come on strong and direct. One of my teammates jokes that when I'm passionate about something, she has to remind the "lion" that she is "not the meat." Now that we know and trust each other at this level, we can laugh. But when someone doesn't know me well, I am aware that my direct, passionate approach can come off as aggressive, and I can be intimidating. I'm not trying to be that way, it just happens. I go fiercely after what I want, and I love to win. That's why I've been so successful in my sales career! But the perception that can create of me in the minds of some is real, and I have to deal with that and accept it too. It's up to me to decide how much energy I want to spend preparing to get my tone, words, and approach right to minimize harm or ensure a positive interaction out of the gate, or cleaning up the mess on the back end.

I have two more examples related to this about finding your truth and standing in your integrity as you consider the feedback you receive.

Acknowledging Opinions and Honoring Your Integrity

Early in my sales career, I traveled around the country speaking to groups of mostly middle-aged men because of the industry I worked in. For one particular event, I was traveling with my boss's boss; let's call him Steve. Steve and I were slated to host a presentation together on the second day of this conference. We prepared and executed the presentation flawlessly and had a little fun in the process. The following morning, we met for breakfast to debrief and discuss. I was excited to talk about all the positive feedback and the leads we got.

When I arrived at the table, I could instantly feel Steve's nervous energy. I was a bit confused as I had anticipated a light, fun, and celebratory conversation about our performance. I let him lead. He started to review the events of the day, and as he continued to work toward what I could tell was something difficult he wanted to share, he started to sweat. Finally, he just came out and said, "Lindsay, you are very nice looking, and when you wear certain things, I fear no one is listening to what you have to say."

I sat there stunned, confused, and embarrassed. He continued, "You are very smart and very engaging, but when you wear certain clothes, it can be distracting and your intelligence can be overlooked. The reason I'm bringing this up is because I overheard some of the men speaking about you in a way I wouldn't want them talking about you. I addressed it, and I care about you enough that I wanted to talk with you about it."

I could tell he was so uncomfortable and so worried he was going to say the wrong thing. But I also knew he was sincere. At first, I became defensive and said in exasperation, "I can't win. No matter what I wear.

It's always 'too' something." He quickly jumped in and said he agreed that it wasn't my issue, but it was reality. He went on to explain that he wasn't telling me this so that I would change what I wore but so that I was aware of how it was perceived.

That interaction taught me so many valuable lessons. First, if we care about and respect someone enough, we will make ourselves uncomfortable enough to sweat and to share what we believe they need to hear out of love and good intentions. Second, I should share feedback to create awareness for someone, not necessarily to direct them to do something different. He did not say, "You shouldn't wear . . ." Instead, he shared, "When you wear . . . this is how it is perceived/this is what happens." He left the decision in my hands. Third, it's up to me to decide and live with the consequences of my decisions. I can wear tight, low-cut clothes and live with the consequences, or I can choose something else and live with those consequences. The trade-offs are mine to make because the consequences are mine to live with, and at the end of the day, I'm the one who has to look at myself in the mirror.

Respecting Differences and Living with Our Choices

When my husband Mitch and I started dating, we quickly found out that we each handled conflict very differently. When we had a disagreement or argument that got heated, I wanted to lean into it and work through it no matter how hot it got, whereas he much preferred to make space to cool off and come back together later to resolve the issue. I was convinced that he was wrong and my way was right. After all, we're always supposed to work toward resolution, right?

Every time we got into it, I continued to pursue him no matter what. Even when he walked into another room, I would follow him. In my previous relationships, I wouldn't let my partners disengage. This typically ended in verbal or physical violence. Mitch wouldn't do that. He would simply shut down, and when I relentlessly pursued, he would calmly but sternly tell me to "stop it" and remind me that if he said anything in that moment, it would be something he'd regret, and he didn't want to do that to me. Not much to say after that.

When we started debriefing on these situations, and I was willing to listen to his side, I realized he genuinely believed that his way of navigating the situation was the right one. I also realized that we were both after the same thing: resolution. We just had different things we were or weren't willing to experience or deal with on the journey to resolution. I wanted to actively work together toward resolution even if we were going to say things out of emotion or frustration that we didn't mean. To me, disengagement felt like abandonment or giving up. I didn't want that and was willing to risk anything to stay engaged. He wanted to make space in the moment, knowing we would reengage, so we wouldn't say anything damaging out of emotion or frustration that we didn't mean.

After discovering this about ourselves, we were able to come up with a way that honored each of our approaches and desires. When he was at a place where he wanted to disengage, I needed him to say that he wanted to come back to this in the next hour, the next day, or whatever his timeline was, so I knew when I could expect us to reengage and not feel abandoned. I needed to let it go in that moment and go on with something else to give him the space he needed to process things and cool off.

It took a few reps for us to break our old habits and remember what we needed to do for each other, but we are in a good groove now. This experience has helped me be better at navigating conflict with friends, family, coworkers, and community members in a way that honors myself and their needs in the process. When we're missing each other or misunderstanding each other, it can be powerful when we ask the other person what expectations and assumptions they are operating from. This opens our eyes to new ways of seeing and understanding things.

In the next chapter, we will bring together a lot of the work we have done thus far and look at the story it tells us about who we are and why we are the way we are. No doubt you have learned things about yourself that invoke the full spectrum of emotions. Now the door is open, and we can see ourselves and the world in a new way. Facing a new reality takes courage. Understanding that new reality and what it means requires deep work. I hope you are ready to take the next steps into understanding and exploring meaning. This is the path to peace, freedom, and love, and it's worth the work. I promise!

If you have started to collect feedback, let's do some additional reflection: How did this feedback shift your perception about yourself, others, and your worldview? Don't jump to conclusions or into action just yet, but stay in the space of working to understand.

REFLECT ON YOUR JOURNEY

- What have you learned, unlearned, or relearned in this chapter?

- What has been most valuable to you?

- What one thing will you commit to doing differently going forward?

- Who can you invite in to keep you accountable?

CHAPTER 6

Facing a New Reality

The self-restoration process, if done with an open heart and open mind, will alter your reality. The way you see yourself, others, and the world will be different. In this process of discovering and exploring, you will see new things and see old things in new ways. I am facing a new reality as I write this chapter, in fact. As I reflected on this past year, I realized that I continue to operate from two key limiting beliefs:

- If things aren't painful and difficult, then I'm not doing enough.
- Listening to my heart and following my intuition will lead me down the wrong path.

I discovered these limiting beliefs and figured out their untruths by going through the process described in the previous chapters. I know these beliefs are holding me back, and that these statements are not true and not serving me, yet my thoughts and behavior are rooted deeply in them. In this chapter, I will share my personal story as support as we walk through the process of transitioning to a new reality, away from and out of the pattern of limiting beliefs. But first, let's take time to explore what new realities you need to face.

So far, we have explored your experiences, beliefs, behaviors, influences, patterns, habits, routines, and feedback from others. These all give you a lot to explore with regard to who you are and why you are the way you are. What new realities do you need to face? In other words, what beliefs, assumptions, expectations, and values have you become aware of that need to be shifted because they are limiting your ability to live and lead in a meaningful and impactful way?

In my work, I encounter many common paradigm shifts that clients wake up to during this process, including the following:

- I need to stop forcing and trying to control everything—especially things I can't, like other people—and allow things to unfold because I don't want to be anxious, exhausted, and angry all the time.

- I need to shift out of a victim mentality and take ownership and responsibility for who I want to be and how I want to live.

- I need to accept my reality and let go of the resentment and frustration of things I wish were different because my energy is consumed by resisting what is and I feel stuck.

- I need to find my self-worth and value outside of my job.

- I need to make time to rest because my addiction to productivity and *doing* is degrading my relationships and quality of life.

- I need to remember that life happens in seasons and cycles, and although I don't particularly enjoy the one I'm in, I know it won't last forever.

- I need to invest in my relationships because I've been trying to do everything on my own for so long and I'm lonely.

- I need to reopen my heart and mind to other people and other ways of doing things because I've been acting out of self-protection and guarding my heart, but now I realize I am safe and I want deeper connections.

- I need to stop worrying about what everyone else thinks about me and what I should be doing and focus on what I know is right for me.

- I need to invite others in and bring others along so we can make faster progress and a deeper impact.

- I need to spend more time thinking, because I'm not getting the right things done at the right time, the quality of what I'm getting done is low, and I'm stretched way too thin.

- I need to stop saying yes to everything that comes my way so that I can stay focused on the most important things and what I feel called and qualified to do to make a bigger impact.

IDENTIFYING YOUR LIMITING BELIEFS

Your turn! Consider what beliefs are causing negative patterns to occur in your life or what beliefs feel negative or heavy. Or maybe you can think of the opposite, a belief you want to hold but seems too good to be true. What is its opposite? For example, maybe you want to believe that people are inherently good, but what you expose yourself to every day tells you differently. The limiting belief you could capture is "People are inherently bad." Again, the purpose of capturing these is to start to identify how those beliefs are shaping your thoughts and actions. Write down two limiting beliefs.

FINDING MEANING

In looking at the limiting beliefs you wrote down, what paradigm shifts were revealed? To think about what's behind these limiting beliefs and to face what's feeding them, you need to answer two questions:

- What does this limiting belief mean?

- What is my new starting place?

Let's walk through this process together using one of my limiting belief examples. The story I often tell myself and keep coming back to is this: "If things aren't painful and difficult, then I'm not doing enough." When I dug deeper into this belief, I discovered that I still subconsciously believe the following secondary limiting beliefs that are driving this narrative:

- Unless something is hard, it must not be worthwhile.

- I do not deserve to enjoy life and work.

- Depletion is a sign that I'm on the right path.

- Being busy and contributing are why people love and value me.

- If I don't push hard enough, I will get soft and weak.

- *Doing*—being productive—is the only value there is in life.

Yikes and yuck! That was painful, and I hate even putting these statements down on paper. I'm filled with guilt and shame looking at these bullets . . . but that's OK. I've learned that in order to release the power of these fears and limiting beliefs and to shift into a healthier way, I must say them out loud or write them down and bring them into the light. I am a work in progress, so I have nothing to be ashamed of. Neither do you. Feel it so you can heal it.

Let's keep using my preceding example and look at the first subconscious belief I uncovered: "Unless something is hard, it must not be worthwhile." Ask yourself what the words *hard* and *worthwhile* mean in this context. Don't go digging out your dictionary—yet. Just write out what the words mean to you. When I read this statement, *hard* means difficult, challenging, exasperating, frustrating, depleting. *Worthwhile* means memorable, worthy of a large investment, significant, meaningful.

Once I've written down what these words mean to me, I look at the statement again. Is it true? What evidence in my life and in history is there for and against this statement? Sure, many inventions, systematic and cultural shifts, books, and humanitarian efforts were very hard and very worthwhile *and* some that were worthwhile were pretty easy and effortless, maybe even happenstance. Even when they were hard, would the people who were in the middle of the work describe *hard* the same way I did?

Thinking this through helps me realize that my all-or-nothing limiting belief around what's hard and worthwhile is holding me back and needs to shift. To make that shift, I have to bring examples of the opposite into my awareness. Spending meaningful time with my grandparents is worthwhile but not hard. Gathering around the dinner table with friends for meaningful conversation and a good meal is worthwhile but not hard. Writing my blog is worthwhile but not hard. Serving others in my volunteer positions is worthwhile but not hard. Sending thank-you notes to people is worthwhile but not hard. Working with individuals, teams, and organizations in their life and leadership journey is worthwhile but not hard as I have defined it.

This exploration helps me get to a deeper truth that lies in my second subconscious limiting belief: "I do not deserve to enjoy life and work." This is a generational, ancestral message that has been deeply ingrained in me from my family. We struggled. Working on or toward something we enjoyed was not an option. Work was a sacrifice made for financial security. Life was more challenging than it was enjoyable. Why should I deserve something that my ancestors didn't have?

Maybe a better question is why wouldn't I honor the chance to pursue an enjoyable life and enjoyable work that allow me to use my gifts to contribute in a bigger way than my ancestors could? Perhaps this is what they have worked so hard for and now I have the chance to live it out on behalf of us all? This feels more in line with the truth that lies in my heart. When I ask my family for their perspective, this is what they tell me. Now it's my work to set aside the guilt and limiting beliefs to face and honor this new reality, and to do the work to shift into a new way of thinking and believing.

EXPLORING YOUR LIMITING BELIEFS

Using your two limiting beliefs, make some space to explore their meaning with the question, "What does this mean?" Define the terms in your limiting belief statements. Consider what additional beliefs are tied to these words (reference my list, if helpful). Knowing the meaning will help as you begin to discover a new starting point and the paradigm shifts you need to make.

DISCOVERING A NEW STARTING POINT

Through my exploration, I uncovered three new starting points—or new realities: "I deserve enjoyment," "I am worthy to receive good," and "Things that are meaningful can be easy and enjoyable." Your new starting points are the truths you have rediscovered or remembered that were always there hiding behind your fear, guilt, shame, ego, or wounds.

All of us have these beliefs and biases that are not true, that are limiting us, and that are founded in our experiences. When we uncover them and write them down, it can trigger even deeper feelings of shame and guilt. "I should have known better" or "How could I honestly believe that?" or "Isn't it obvious?" In writing mine out for you, I have all those same thoughts and accompanying feelings.

Then I remind myself that I am imperfect and on a constant learning journey. Now I know, and I can move forward. Writing down these beliefs may also bring up sentiments like, "Do I really deserve this?" and "What about all the times I was bad?" or "This feels and sounds so selfish." Again, I am not only writing these as examples of how you could feel but also because this is exactly how I feel reading what I've written down.

DISCOVERING YOUR NEW REALITIES

What new realities do you need to face? You may wind up with a list as long as the one representing my clients that I included toward the beginning of the chapter. Remember that there will always be new layers to uncover and new things to work on. I've said it before and I'll say it again: This is a lifelong journey. Pace yourself! Pick the top one or two new realities that strike you and write them down. There is no one right way to do this. Simply write down whatever comes to your heart and mind.

DEVELOPING SKILLS TO LIVE OUT A NEW REALITY

Just because we have come to awareness, and even if we have moved on to understanding, that doesn't mean we can make the leap to acceptance.

That may take time and some new skill development. I know that it will for me!

So, on to the next question: *What skills or practices do I need to develop to live this out?*

If we go back to the common "I need" paradigm shift statements earlier in this chapter, a number of skills come up that could apply for us. Examples include creating a reflection practice, making time to listen, developing a habit of letting go, getting comfortable in the unknown, allowing things to fall apart, and embracing change.

In looking again at my limiting belief example and what I dug up to determine its meaning, I need to hone my skills for receiving good and accepting enjoyment. If I go back to the reframing of my own situation, my family has given me a gift that I am refusing to receive, and I am therefore blocking the acceptance of any enjoyment I could have. I am refusing it because I don't like to owe people anything, I don't want my family to think that I believe I'm better than them, and deep down, I don't know why I am worthy of this gift.

Again, as I look back at what I have written, it seems silly. My family doesn't expect anything in return, other than that I love and respect them, which I do and always will. I will do everything in my power not to create the perception that I believe I am better than anyone—ever—especially my family, and yet that is not something I can control. If they want to think that, no matter what I do, they will. I have to let that go and continue to let it go when comments are made that feed that limiting belief.

Finally, I know in my heart that I am a good person and I will steward anything given to me in life and work well because I have put in the work to become healthier, more aware of my impact on others and the world, and more intentional about where I put my energy and what matters most. I am doing the best I can, and that's what I can do. That gives me the confidence to know I am worthy of this gift.

I'm moving toward acceptance, but I still need to work on the skills and practices of accepting enjoyment and receiving good. So what does that look like for me in practical terms? How will I actually develop these skills and practices? My primary fear in accepting enjoyment and receiving good is that I will become selfish and lazy—that if I enjoy too much or get comfortable with the good, it will make me a person I don't want to become. I also feel guilt around why I should receive enjoyment and good when so many are suffering. And I believe that if I keep myself from fully enjoying things, I won't be perceived as better than others and won't have to feel bad.

I know in my head these fears are not real. The first fear won't come into reality because my friends, family, and I, myself, would never let that happen. The second fear is rooted in a lie and scarcity mindset. Enjoyment is not like pie to be divided out—if I get some, then there's less for you. There is an unlimited supply for each of us if we choose it. That fear is also rooted in the lie that people who enjoy things are perceived as better than someone who is struggling or doesn't enjoy things.

To develop the skills and practices that will create my new reality, I first need to catch myself accepting enjoyment and receiving good. Then, through reflection, I need to consider how doing those things is changing me in a positive or negative way. I have to "prove" that I can accept enjoyment and receive good to accept and live my new reality. To do that, I focus on keeping a journal of the good I receive and how it makes me feel and act. I also notice the times when I am enjoying the moment and then catch myself pulling back from it and push myself back into full enjoyment. I journal and reflect on those moments at the end of the day too, and notice how they change the way I feel and act. Once I have done this practice for a period of time, this new reality will become the only one that I believe and live from.

IDENTIFYING SKILLS AND PRACTICES

So far, you have identified your limiting beliefs, explored their meaning, and stated your new realities. Now, we put all of this into action by understanding what skills or practices you need to develop to live out these new realities. Consider my examples as you make your own list. Knowing is the first step; adjusting your actions makes this real and is required for positive change in your life and leadership.

Here are some examples to get you thinking:

- Creating a reflection practice
- Making time to listen
- Receiving good
- Accepting enjoyment
- Being vulnerable
- Opening back up
- Developing a habit of letting go
- Getting comfortable in the unknown
- Allowing things to fall apart
- Embracing change
- Accepting yourself and your life for what they are
- Pausing before speaking or reacting
- Getting present
- Preparing for your day
- Discerning the information you take in
- Journaling about your experiences and feelings
- Practicing gratitude

If you are an open-hearted achiever like me, you have been all in on this process and identified several skills and practices you could develop to help you on your journey. Please choose one. For a skill or practice to become fully developed, it needs the time and attention it deserves.

LIVING IN ALIGNMENT AND INTEGRITY

Many of us have a deeper issue to address, which is that we cannot do this work sustainably until we are living in alignment and integrity. I have said this statement before—"I am doing the best I can, and that's what I can do"—to shift my limiting beliefs and open myself up to abundance, but there was always a piece of my heart and spirit that resisted it as untrue. Because it was untrue. I said all the right things and had the right intentions, but I wasn't willing to put in the work to align my heart, mind, and spirit. I wanted to believe it, but I know I wasn't doing what I needed to for it to be true and to be in my integrity.

As I have continued to do this work on increasing my awareness, healing, and becoming more intentional, that resistance has continued to lessen. I can confidently say that statement now and know that it is true. I've had to make sacrifices and difficult shifts, and as new things pop up, I have to continue to work at it. Some of the skills I've acquired in my journey and continue to develop are releasing judgment, walking away from gossip, saying no when I need to (versus saying yes out of obligation and being resentful), delaying gratification, making the decision that is best for my health versus giving in to temptations, getting up early to get the quiet time I need to prepare to show up as my best self for the day by:

- Praying and asking for forgiveness
- Practicing gratitude
- Focusing on what I have versus what I don't

Now when I feel resistance to that statement, it's more of a gut check on whether I can say it honestly based on what I know and where I am. Sometimes in that check an opportunity to realign is revealed, and other times it is simply a confirmation that I can accept and receive. If

I don't walk myself through this process, I will subconsciously block myself from these gifts, but when I bring that statement to my conscious awareness and allow myself to honestly check in, I open myself up to acceptance and receiving.

SHIFTING BACK INTO ALIGNMENT

Are there areas of your life where you feel out of alignment or out of your integrity? List those now. Prioritize them according to frequency or impact.

Decide how you will keep these areas top of mind, so you can make progress on shifting them. Keep them in a list on a mirror or even in your journal so you can check in, either daily or weekly, and see how you are doing. This practice can be powerful!

ACCEPTING YOUR PLACE IN THE JOURNEY

Each of us is on our own healing journey, and we are at different stages in that journey. Your physical age isn't much of a factor. I know teenagers who are pretty advanced, and people close to the end of their life who are just starting out. Advancement on the journey has less to do with knowledge or experience and more to do with a willingness to be open-hearted and open-minded; a willingness to see yourself—the good, the bad, and the ugly—in an honest way; a willingness to face your fears and the things you have been hiding from, running from, or burying down deep; and a willingness to explore the meaning of your life.

As you navigate through your new realities, it can feel as if your entire foundation has been taken out from under you. What you thought you knew for sure—your view of the world—has been changed. You are starting from a new place that is foreign, unknown, and unsettling. Be patient with yourself. Stay in the discomfort. I described it to my coach as feeling like a balloon that is floating in the wind, barely tethered. Like, at any moment, everything I have known will disappear. I can't see the ground, and I'm am not sure which way is up. Yep, super uncomfortable. Trust me, as time goes on, the ground will reappear, and you will see the same world in a whole new way. The worst thing we can do is convince ourselves to revert back to the old way.

ESTABLISHING SUPPORT

What support do you need to stay on track through this part of your restoration process? Who could you reach out to and invite in to support you? What positive affirmations or routines could you put in place that will prevent you from giving up or reverting back to old ways?

UNIVERSAL REALITIES FOR US ALL

I want to provide a few universal truths or realities—some may be new to you—to help you stay anchored while you are going through this process. The first and most powerful is the only reality that matters: you were created to love and be loved. In fact, you are love. This is important to keep in mind because it guards you against shame and guilt as you let go of your old realities and discover new ones. Well, maybe you rediscover and remember them! For most of us, we know these realities to be true, but our egos and protections have convinced us otherwise. The fact that you were created to love and be loved also helps you stay open and be compassionate with yourself as you navigate. Fear can shut us down and make us want to quit. When we remember that we are love, in light of everything, we drive out that fear and continue our healing and forward progress.

Another universal reality to keep in mind is that you are imperfect and that's just as it should be. That's why you are loved as much as you are. For your imperfections. There is no such thing as a perfect human, and there never will be. None of us has this figured out, and the healing journey never ends. There are and always will be things we can do better and work toward. Don't compare yourself to others because your comparison gauge is not accurate. We will perceive others as perfect and like they have it all figured out, but it's just not true. And even if, by some miracle, they do have it all together in that moment, life happens, and it all falls apart. That's just how it goes. This is a difficult but also freeing reality to acknowledge and accept.

Notice the lies still present in my life after years of this work. New things happen, new experiences are had, and all we can do is see the lies and know what to do about them. They will continue to come into our minds but with less frequency and intensity. We will continue to accelerate the shifts, so we are making decisions and living from our highest self. That's all we can do.

A TIP FOR IMPLEMENTING YOUR NEW SKILLS AND PRACTICES

I have a tendency to think that if I implement several things fairly well, I will get further faster, and I prove to myself time and again this is not the right approach. One of my business teammates likes to remind me that consistency matters more than intensity, especially when we are working to integrate something that results in a long-lasting, deep-heart mindset and behavioral shift.

The skill or practice you choose will become integrated into who you are and will simply be something, like brushing your teeth, that you just do over time without thinking about it. Sometimes with our skills and practices, there is no end we can reach but we have to keep investing in and practicing them. They are not skills that can be mastered and we just stop doing. For instance, I've incorporated a letting-go practice into my life. There are times when I get hurried or too busy, and I stop practicing letting go. Even though I'm in a much better spot today than I was a year ago, when I don't do that practice, I slip back into the stressful, anxious Lindsay of five years ago. The letting-go practice is required if I want to stay in my new reality and operate from my highest self. Period.

Choose your skill or practice, tell a buddy, and get to work. Don't forget to reflect on or document the changes you see and feel so you can maintain the desire to stick to it!

REFLECT ON YOUR JOURNEY

- What have you learned, unlearned, or relearned in this chapter?
- What has been most valuable to you?
- What one thing will you commit to doing differently going forward?
- Who can you invite in to keep you accountable?

CHAPTER 7

Surrendering and Releasing

With every change or transformation, there is a beginning, a middle, and an end. I don't know about you, but I hate endings, and I'm no good at them. I suppose that most of us aren't. Endings come with finality and sometimes feelings of grief. They usually require surrendering and releasing, which is why we will spend some time here. These are things we are taught from a young age to actively avoid, so we don't know how to do it.

Let's start this exploration with an example from my journey and then you can take the space you need to consider how to navigate this step of surrendering and releasing. As you learned in the previous chapter, I held an old reality—"If things aren't painful and difficult, then I'm not doing enough"—that I shifted to new ones: "I deserve enjoyment," "I am worthy to receive good," and "Things that are meaningful can be easy and enjoyable." To get to my new starting point, there was a lot between my old reality and the new realities that I needed to surrender and release.

A PROCESS FOR SURRENDER AND RELEASE

Guilt and shame came up during the shifting process that I needed to release: wishing that I would have learned this sooner, that I should have known better, or that this could have been different. I had to *surrender to* those thoughts, meaning I had to acknowledge and accept them instead of ignoring or running from them, and also *surrender* them, meaning I had to stop resisting or trying to control them and allow them to exist. These two steps of surrendering allow and enable you to release your thoughts and feelings, to lay them down and move through them to ultimately be free of them. It took me a long time to recognize the many ways I can successfully surrender and release my thoughts and feelings. In practicing this process, I also learned that surrendering and releasing is not a one-time thing; it's something I often have to do over and over and over before I am completely free of the weight of the thought or feeling. There are a few different scenarios and ways of working through the surrender and release process that I want to walk you through. First, you have to become aware of a particular thought and your feelings around it.

Scenario 1: Recognizing my thought and rewriting it helps shift my thoughts and feelings.

Recognizing a thought means increasing your awareness and slowing down to notice it. When a thought comes into my mind, I catch it and hold it there. "I should have known better." Then I speak truth to myself, whether in my mind or out loud, reminding myself that things couldn't have been different, I couldn't have known better, and although maybe I could have learned this sooner, I didn't, and there's nothing I can do about that. This process of becoming aware of my thought, catching it, and reminding myself of the truth makes me aware that I'm stuck in the past and expending precious energy where it is simply wasted. Talking myself through this is usually enough to make the shift to surrendering feelings of guilt or shame, but sometimes, those feelings still linger long after the thoughts have shifted and are released.

Scenario 2: Recognizing my thought and rewriting it shifts my thoughts but not my feelings.

When I need more effort than just recognizing my thoughts and feelings to get to release, I am challenged to befriend my feelings, acknowledge them, get curious about them, and have compassion for myself. At this point, I am past trying to figure out why I feel the way I feel. That doesn't help much. In fact, the question of *why* can keep us stuck in an unproductive loop of guilt and shame, trying to figure out what is not logically *figure-outable*. We may never understand why we feel the feelings we feel, but understanding is not required for us to make a shift to surrendering those feelings and coming to a better place.

My process looks something like this: I stop what I'm doing and come back fully into my body by closing my eyes and taking three deep breaths (this is part of the reconnection exercise we went through in Chapter 1; we always start with connection). If I feel settled, I literally talk to those feelings. "Shame, I know you're here. I feel you. I don't understand why you are here, but I'm not upset about it. Is there something you have to teach me?" I know, I know. This sounds very woo-woo. Trust me, I thought the same thing until I started actively participating in it and witnessed the results. That act of acknowledging and opening up, releasing resistance and frustration about the feeling, and allowing yourself to feel it could be enough for it to release.

Scenario 3: Recognizing my thought and rewriting it doesn't shift my thoughts or feelings.

There are times when those first two steps don't work, especially early in your journey when you don't know what the shift feels like and you don't yet believe that you have the power to make these shifts, to surrender and release. In those scenarios, something more active can help. I don't have all the answers, and you have to find what works for you, but here are a couple of ideas of what works for me.

Write it out. If I'm stuck in a loop where the thought and feelings won't go away, then I go deeper into them. Sounds absurd inside a culture that promotes avoiding and distracting ourselves from any of our thoughts and feelings. Most of us have bought into the lie that if we just go do something else, the thoughts and feelings will eventually go away. Wrong. They will stay stuck inside you, possibly even changing form to unrecognizable anger or frustration . . . but they will burst out at somebody someday.

The worst is when we let our thoughts and feelings pile up for years and years and years, and they become a giant, jumbled hairball we can't decipher. All we know is that we feel like crap, and we don't know why. We have no clue where to start, and we have to start pulling one string at a time to unwind it all. Trust me, this takes years of therapy, so if this is you, start today! Don't let any more strings accumulate in your jumbled hairball! Don't think it's worth the effort? Wrong again, my friend. You will not feel free and at peace until you take it all apart. It's worth every ounce of energy you have if you want to live a life where peace, hope, and love are present.

Back to writing it out. Let it flow. Write down whatever comes into your mind and heart. What are you thinking? How are you feeling? Let it flow freely all over the page. Don't try to make it make sense. This way of writing helps you get to some of the unconscious and subconscious thoughts that lie at the root of what needs to shift. Letting them out and allowing them to see the light instead of staying stuck in the dark corners and shadows can be what you need to shift your thoughts and feelings. If the writing alone doesn't give you that release, go back and read what you wrote. Reflecting on what you put down on paper in black and white can be another powerful way for you to make the thoughts and feelings shift.

Walk, run, or work it out. If writing it out is not working, try getting physical. After all, thoughts and feelings are energy. Keep the thoughts and feelings front and center in your mind as you walk, run, or work out. Allow the physical movement of your body to process what you are thinking and feeling. This works especially well for me when I'm thinking in a violent or hateful way and feeling angry or defensive (hurt or resentful, actually, since anger is my go-to cover-up emotion).

I will never forget one time when I was so angry that I thought I might vibrate out of my body. I knew I needed to drop everything and get to the gym, or I was literally going to punch the next person that looked at me wrong. I kept my head down and earbuds in as I entered the gym and went straight for the treadmill (because there was no punching bag, or I would have unloaded on that thing). I cranked the treadmill up to ten, which is way faster than I would ever even think about running and far past where I'm comfortable, but I knew my body needed to be pushed to an all-out sprint for this energy to be released. What's wild is that I kept running at that pace for several minutes before I could feel the energy dissipating and start to shift. It was like an out-of-body experience, like it wasn't really me.

When I reached exhaustion and my legs could no longer keep up, I stopped the treadmill and stumbled back to a quiet corner in the stretching room. Once I caught my breath, I completely broke down. I was bawling and couldn't stop it. That anger had turned to hurt and that hurt was flooding out of my eyes. I let that go on for the time it needed to, and I felt the tenderness of that experience shift my thoughts and my feelings about the entire situation. I settled down, pulled myself back together, and walked out of the gym with a smile on my face. That is the power physical activity can have on helping us surrender and release our thoughts and feelings.

ADDITIONAL PRACTICES AND TOOLS FOR SURRENDER AND RELEASE

If you don't have the physical ability to work out those thoughts and feelings, other tools are available to you. One available to us all is breathing. Slow four-plus-count breaths or even rapid breathing. You can focus on the breathing itself, or you can think about your uncomfortable thoughts and feelings going out when you breathe out, and pleasant, peaceful thoughts and feelings coming in when you breathe in. Another way is through music, whether simply listening to it, swaying to it, or actually dancing to it (no matter how silly you look). When it feels right, I turn on a sad song when I'm sad and just let myself cry. I allow myself to be completely overcome by the emotions, and it's only in that place of being flooded by them, forced to surrender, where I am able to release them and shift. When it feels right, I turn on heavy metal and jump and dance until I'm sweaty. Other times I'm called to a rhythmic beat, and I allow my arms and legs to move without worrying about anyone seeing me. It's so freeing!

You can include other people to help you surrender and release your thoughts and feelings when you just can't get there on your own. Being held or hugged for an extended time has worked for me. You can also talk with someone about the situation, if you are willing to share. Allowing them to help you see another perspective or to rewrite and positively affirm you is another healthy way to make a shift.

Use these examples to start thinking about other methods that could support your surrender and release journey. There isn't one right way. The point is that you get to a place where you stop resisting and surrender by acknowledging and accepting that thought and feeling, because only in doing so will it be released. You may have to take a few extra steps to get to full surrender or from surrender to release, but the point is that you get free of those thoughts and feelings.

SURRENDER AND RELEASE WITH OTHERS INVOLVED

Working through surrender and release when it's your own self-inflicted thoughts and feelings is one thing, but how do you move through surrender and release when someone else is involved—someone you don't have control over, someone whose actions you can't change and whose words you can't erase, someone who won't even speak to you or attempt to apologize or reconcile? Oh boy, this is a toughie.

I've been there. And I still find myself there today. Some have been minor misunderstandings and disagreements, and some have been so large that I had myself convinced that I could never move on or forgive if we weren't able to have a reconciliation conversation. But then, that time never came, and I was still angry, resentful, and very hurt. I was faced with the reality that in order for me to get to a place of peace, I would have to find a way through surrender and release without an apology, without acknowledgment of wrongdoing or the pain caused, without any reconciliation. So I want to offer some guidance on how I have and continue to move through this process of surrender and release when there are others involved, and provide some exercises that have helped me on my journey.

A couple things to note before we jump in: 1) We always have a decision on whether we want to include the other person in our surrender and release process and should consider the consequences of both ways, and 2) even if we include the other person in the journey, we are responsible for surrender and release no matter how they participate in our process.

SURRENDERING OLD WOUNDS AND RELEASING NEGATIVE EMOTIONS

In college, I considered majoring in political science. I was always interested in social change, and some of my favorite people to read about who inspired me were prominent leaders who had influenced major social systems, often through politics, in courageous ways. When I shared this dream with a particular family member, his immediate response was: "You may want to rethink your plans. No one would ever take a pretty blonde like you seriously in politics." Initially, I was shocked by his response. When the shock wore off, I slipped into anger and contempt. At the same time, as I was experiencing those emotions, I was allowing a reality to be created for me. This off-handed comment turned into a lie I would play over and over and start to believe—to the point that I allowed it to creep in and build doubt so large I didn't see another way forward except to change my major.

I went another direction, and those words haunted my thoughts. The feelings stayed with me for years. Long after I graduated from college, I still felt them. If I'm honest, I still struggle today with uncomfortable feelings toward this person for those comments, and I'm still working on surrender and release twenty years later. However, those thoughts and feelings have shifted. I no longer believe those words to be true. When those thoughts enter my mind now, I immediately recognize them as a lie, and my heart softens and settles. Anger and contempt have been replaced by irritation and disappointment (less emotionally charged). Where I felt personally attacked before, I now see ignorance and insecurity on this person's part, and I know it's not about me—it's about so much more than me.

I have never confronted the person about this situation for a couple of reasons. First, I don't think he would even recall saying it. Not even the day after. It's so ingrained in his nature to put people down that he probably didn't put much thought into what he said at all and certainly wouldn't perceive it as being harmful. Second, if I attempted to tell him how I felt or ask for an apology, I truly believe he would argue, deflect, and deny, possibly even try to turn it around on me. I've seen him do it multiple times to others. He has no interest in seeing someone else's point of view and does not have the mental or emotional maturity to take responsibility for his actions. If I attempted to talk with him about it, he would be mad, I would get frustrated, and I'd *still* be stuck with the same thoughts and feelings.

To move on from this in the short term, I used some of the techniques mentioned earlier, and I wrote him letters that shared how I really felt but that I knew I would never send. I went at that paper without holding anything back. I wrote things I definitely would never want anyone to read, and in giving myself permission to write them down, surrendering to the anger, those feelings started to shift, and I could see the thoughts shift too. I recognized that he was a sad, insecure man whose comments may have been directed at me but weren't really about me. They consisted of years of pent-up frustration after being rejected by women, and even though I was family, I wasn't immune from the nastiness his insecurities brought out.

In my relationship with my dad, I experienced multiple traumatic wounds inflicted over a period of years. In the time since, it has not been possible to have a conversation that could lead to reconciliation. The pain, lies, and limiting beliefs these experiences created in my being have been profound. I will be healing from them for the rest of my life.

For years, I blamed him for every bad thing that happened to me. I was consumed by anger and defensiveness, which masked the deep worry I felt; wondering if I was broken, unlovable, and unworthy. This anger and defensiveness covered up the hurt that my little child's heart felt and the unfathomable confusion I experienced. Surrendering to and releasing the thoughts and feelings associated with these experiences seemed impossible. When I came to the realization that there was little to no possibility of acknowledging or discussing in hopes of reconciling, I faced a tough decision. I could stay beholden to these thoughts and feelings, or I could choose to heal and move on. My dad did not want to participate in the process, but that didn't mean that I couldn't continue the journey of healing on my own, and that eventually we could forge our relationship in a new way.

I used all of the following exercises to do my own healing on my journey, and I continue to use them today. I'm happy to report that with persistence and dedication, the feelings of anger have gone. The lies around brokenness, unworthiness, and unlovability have continued to transform, and my dad and I can see each other at family gatherings and converse normally. I see the entire situation and each of us who played a part in a different light now. After allowing myself to fully surrender to the feelings I had been hiding and avoiding for most of my life, after allowing the pain to consume me, I have become freer and more at peace. I have come back to love for myself and for all the people involved.

The following exercises can be used for everyday situations and are effective for those bigger, more complex situations. They help us remember what we can and cannot control, pull us out of a victim mentality, and help us see clearly what we have a responsibility to take ownership of to improve our situation. These exercises move past the mental and emotional processing and invite us into a deeper level of spiritual surrender and release.

THE SERENITY PRAYER

The power of prayer is real when you allow yourself to be fully present. This one is particularly powerful and used in the famous twelve-step program because it invites you to recognize and release what isn't yours to carry, inspires you to take action where you have responsibility, and encourages you to reflect regularly to know where those lines are. Simply speaking these words to yourself over and over can have a profound effect on your mental and emotional state.

God, grant me the serenity to accept the things I cannot change, the courage to change the things I can, and the wisdom to know the difference.

PUSH EXERCISE TO RELEASE FRUSTRATION AND ANGER TOWARD SOMEONE

This exercise can be particularly helpful when you have had an intense interaction with an individual that has left you feeling angry, betrayed, resentful, or experiencing another strong emotion. It gives you the release you desire from an emotional standpoint and also reminds you to let go of what you cannot control (which is the other person) and invite God in to heal the relationship.

Picture the person you are angry with or frustrated by. The two of you are on a cliff, and you are walking them back to the edge. Imagine yourself pushing that person off the cliff (this will provide you with an emotional release) but into God's hands (this signifies that you are releasing judgment and responsibility to God and freeing yourself of it).

FORGIVENESS PRAYER

Forgiveness is one of the hardest and best things you can do to bring peace and freedom to your life. It's easy to blame others for what has happened to you or even what you have done, but that keeps you from wholeness. It leaves you stuck. Use this forgiveness prayer when you don't know where to start or what else to do, even when it's only to forgive yourself.

God, please forgive [name] for [action].
I forgive [name] for [action].
God, please also forgive me for any ill will or negative action on my part in this situation and relationship.
I forgive myself for my ill will and negative action.

The Difficult Practice of Forgiveness

A couple notes on forgiveness. In my own journey, I was often so focused on whether the person deserved forgiveness that I didn't always realize I was keeping myself stuck in an unhealthy pattern and negative emotions. Forgiveness has little to do with the other person and has everything to do with you. It greatly impacts your well-being. It allows you to take your power and energy back, so you can live, think, and act with freedom and peace, able to be fully present for other things.

Since I have started my own business, I have been betrayed time and time again. This has looked like everything from people making commitments and not following through, to stealing my ideas and passing them off as their own, to falsely accusing me of things and attempting to damage my reputation, and everything in between. Early on, I would hold on to those wrongdoings with anger and resentment, but I could always feel this pulling me into a closed-off scarcity mindset, meaning I was operating out of fear, desiring control, and thinking about everything I was not. I was defensive and unhappy.

As I have worked through surrender and release using all the tools in this chapter, I have been able to stay open and confident in the face of these kinds of arrows being launched my way. I realized that shutting down and getting defensive were exactly what my attackers wanted me to do. They were trying to intimidate me and make me small. By fighting back or holding a grudge, I was allowing them to win. Forgiving them and rising above allowed me to keep moving forward, focus on better things, and experience the freedom I needed to pursue my own path. Their arrows couldn't knock me off track; instead, they actually strengthened me.

Maintaining Our Integrity in Forgiveness

Just because I forgive doesn't mean I am naïve or that I forget. I surrendered and released the negative thoughts and emotions, and I put appropriate boundaries in place to protect me going forward. Depending on how hurtful and egregious the attack, those boundaries looked different. In some cases, it was simply agreeing to disagree and moving on. In other cases, it was blocking someone on social media, requesting they no longer contact me in any way, or actively staying away from places where they might be. Over time, some of those hard boundaries loosened, and the other party and I could come together again in a new way. However, some of those boundaries may always need to be in place.

I am careful about the amount of access I grant and the responsibility I put in the hands of another. If they have shown me they can be trusted and will follow through, then I grant more access. If they haven't, I limit my access and the responsibility I give. When I meet someone new, I evaluate how much access and responsibility I give according to my faith in them and willingness to be let down. This helps me protect myself while remaining open to everyone. I don't close all access. Everyone is allowed access, but their behavior dictates how much they get.

This is an important part of our healing and restoration process. Most of us have shut others out and ourselves down to a point where we won't allow ourselves to surrender, which means those negative thoughts and emotions that are holding us back can't be released. This requires courage and vulnerability on your part. You may have to relearn this. For people like me who were wounded early by people tasked with protecting them, you likely shut others out and yourself down at a very early age. You may not even remember what it's like to be open and vulnerable. Start safely with surrendering and releasing on your own. Once you've felt your way through that process, then move into those spaces where you want to include others in the surrender and release process. We have to move through the darkness to get to the light. We have to allow this restoration to take place.

REACHING THE PEAK OF RECONNECTION

And now we've come to the end of Part 1. Congratulations on making it through the most difficult part of the journey. In making it this far, you have climbed to the highest peak. You are exposed and vulnerable, but that's a good thing—it makes you stronger, more aware, and more present than you've ever been. With this new understanding of who you are and why you are the way you are, we are going to move into Part 2, which is all about restoring your intentions.

When people jump to this next part before doing the challenging, foundational work of Part 1, they run the risk of setting intentions that are rooted in old beliefs, patterns, and perceptions that don't really serve them, heal them, or help them step into their fullest potential. We could liken it to dreaming about our ideal self and ideal life without knowing who we are or ideally want to be. This is what most of us do by default without really recognizing it. We just follow the narrative presented to us by culture or those around us.

If you were true and honest about the work in Part 1, you have a new understanding of yourself that will make for a powerful Part 2. That said, the only way to know you have done good work in Part 1 is to check in with your heart. There is no other scorecard but your own integrity. Did you answer the questions to the best of your ability? Did you face things you'd rather avoid? Were you uncomfortable? Do you feel ready to take this new understanding and start to envision the best version of yourself and your life? If so, let's go!

REFLECT ON YOUR JOURNEY

- What have you learned, unlearned, or relearned in this chapter?

- What has been most valuable to you?

- What one thing will you commit to doing differently going forward?

- Who can you invite in to keep you accountable?

PART 2

Restoring Intention

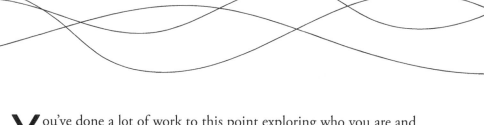

You've done a lot of work to this point exploring who you are and why you are the way you are. You've gone back through your past to discover how your experiences created the thoughts, beliefs, and patterns in your life. You have evaluated what it all means and which of these thoughts, beliefs, and patterns are true and serving you well and which are not. I hope you've been able to surrender and release those that are limiting you or holding you back and have already found some peace and freedom in the process.

Through this new lens of who you are, in this section of the book we will start to explore your present reality and what you want for your future. With those fears and limiting beliefs at bay, we can paint a beautiful picture of who you want to be now and in the future. We will create a solid foundation of understanding as well as new ways of thinking, believing, and doing through the next few chapters before we move into an action plan. Restoring our intention is all about recalibrating our desires and expanding our vision.

In most facets of our life and work, when we set intentions and goals, it's at the request of someone else. We don't take a lot of time to consider what we really want to do and who we really want to be. I want to provide you with the tools and resources in this chapter to do just that—to be who you want to be and live, lead, and work in a way that is true to you. Contrary to what we are taught, there isn't one right way to live or one right way to lead. You've likely been focused on how everyone else is telling you to live and lead. In this section, I want you to do some work asking your inner teacher what they have to say.

THE CHALLENGE OF FACING OUR TRUE SELF

Although this process can be fun, it's not easy. When I start this journey with clients, they have a lot of reservations about saying out loud the things that are in the depths of their heart and soul. An answer comes up, something real, and they hesitate to say it out loud. Others reason an answer away because it doesn't make sense or it's too far from their current reality. I invite you to create a safe space for yourself to open up and allow anything that comes up just to come. You don't necessarily have to do anything about what comes to you. Just bring it into your awareness and see what it has to offer or tell you.

I had a male client who came to me saying he felt stuck and unfulfilled in life and in work, despite having a wonderful marriage and family and a lot of success in his career. He wanted to coach together to find out how to get unstuck and discover what was at the root of his discontent. When we started exploring some of the questions I'll share with you in Chapter 8, we realized that what he had originally thought was meaningful and valuable to him—money, status, achieving at work—didn't matter so much to him anymore. In our time together, he became brave enough to say out loud that despite his success, he thought he might be in the wrong line of work.

As soon as he said it, I saw his energy change and watched him close back up. I could see the regret on his face as he started to explain away what he said. When he was finished, I asked him how long he had been holding that possibility inside himself. He told me he'd been thinking about it for a few years but was too scared to admit it because his current job was all he'd ever done and all that he knew. His career had become such a major part of his identity. If he didn't have that, what did he have? He also shared that he was scared to say it out loud because he was afraid if someone else knew, he would actually have to do something about it.

This theme comes up over and over again with clients in different versions and storylines. We have an inkling about something, but we shove it down or away. We ignore it and hope that it fades. When it doesn't, we convince ourselves there must be something wrong with us. We deny our intuition time and time again, and this causes us to fall into a disconnected, discontented state. What we want and what we get, what is meaningful and what we put our energy into become two different things.

OUR NEED FOR RESTORED, REAL, AND INTENTIONAL LEADERS

People need to learn to listen to their intuition again, their inner teacher, even if they choose not to do anything with what they discover. We need to acknowledge what we're drawn and called to, even if we don't act on it. This choice alone can relieve the disconnected and discontented feelings. Relearning to listen to our intuition, heart, soul, calling, God, whatever you may call it, is required if we want to live a fulfilling and meaningful life. Yes, we may have to come face-to-face with some hard realities we've been ignoring, but on the other hand, once we have started to consider our own needs and desires again, we can look more deeply and expansively to create a greater vision for what's possible in our lives.

During these next few chapters, we will allow ourselves to freely explore things we never have, consider possibilities, and redefine success for our own life, leadership, and work. In the midst of this exploration, we will start to trust ourselves again and rediscover our confidence and our authentic style of leadership. We will see ourselves in a new way and realize gifts we have that others don't. We will identify callings and passions that matter to us. It is at this intersection of our gifts, our passions, and the needs of the world where we can truly serve and shine in the way we were created to!

As we close out Part 2 of this book, we will then consider what we will or won't do about all of these new revelations, what considerations we need to make, and who we could invite into our journey. As a reminder, that client I mentioned said a lot of things during this process that gave him peace. He came to realize why he felt unfulfilled some days and struggled, but he chose to continue down the path he was on. After walking through how his life would be different and the impacts his choices would have on him and those around him, he decided that he didn't want to make the trade-offs required of him to go another direction. He was confident in that decision and the discontentment faded. We each live our own lives and have to decide what is best for us.

Let's dive into your present and future and see what we find!

CHAPTER 8

Exploring What Is Meaningful and Valuable

The first time my coach asked me what was meaningful and valuable to me, I answered the question without hesitation and without anticipation of the realizations and revelations that would follow. It was our second session. I assumed it was a "get to know you" type of question, but it wound up being so much deeper than that. I shared that my faith, my family, and my friends—in that order—were most important to me. Then he asked me the question that turned everything upside down, "If your faith is most important to you, how much time and energy are you investing in it?"

I felt the heat of defensiveness and embarrassment wash over me. I wasn't expecting this to reveal something I needed to address. I'd thought it was just a simple conversation. Moments like these are why most people avoid coaching. You are stretched. Things are reflected back to you in a way you never saw before. For someone like me who always wants to be right, I often feel found out or called out in these moments. I have gotten better about this over time, but I still have to resist the defensiveness that rises up in me and remind myself that's exactly what I pay my coach to do: challenge me and offer new perspectives to consider.

When my coach asked me about how much time and energy I was investing in my faith, I felt these things because I could see where he was going. I had been honest, and I wasn't aligned. Although uncomfortable, this was exactly why I decided to work with this particular coach. I wanted these misalignments and misperceptions to be revealed and brought into the light to be restored. He was curious, kind, compassionate, and gentle with me when he witnessed that I was feeling uncomfortable and exposed, yet he pushed me to process and work through the answer.

What I revealed was that my faith, my number one priority, was getting the leftovers of my time and energy. So were my family and friends, if I was being completely honest. I prioritized work over everything, and anything else just got what was left. What my coach walked me through next was an exercise to expand my thinking and consider what my life would look like in practical terms if my faith, family, and friends were made to be my first priority. It forced me to consider how my schedule, practices, and routines would change if I put those things first and allowed work to get the leftovers. I resisted this exercise right out of the gate, without even being willing to attempt it, but because of my coach's constant and consistent challenge to me that it was possible and that I needed to work through it, I eventually did it. I considered what *ideal* would look like for me in that faith bucket. What practices and habits would I have in place? How would I spend my time and energy if I was actually putting it first and doing it well?

THINKING BIGGER ABOUT WHAT'S POSSIBLE AND WHAT MATTERS

In forcing ourselves to take a big leap out of where we are today, past the microadjustments we could make for incremental changes to our ultimate vision for success, we can see what's really possible. We can expand our possibilities and vision. We can see what it could look and feel like.

Most of us don't take that big leap because we get stuck in *how* to make it possible or *why* it isn't possible. Don't get lost in that. Doing this expansive exercise to create a vision, no matter how seemingly unrealistic, makes us more committed to making the changes that will be required to get just one step closer to our ideal life. It also helps us see that the small steps we will be committing to are nothing compared to the profound and sweeping changes we would need to make to go from where we are today to our ideal state tomorrow. I wish you could have seen what my ideal calendar looked like when I put faith, family, and friends first and let work fill in the gaps. No wonder I was feeling so unfulfilled!

How about you? Have you ever thought about what's meaningful and valuable to you? Common answers for what matters most to people include faith, family, friends, health (mental, emotional, physical, spiritual), fitness, finances, the environment, and social justice. Common answers for what people value most include peace, well-being, balance, happiness, joy, love, justice, respect, a good marriage, downtime, alone time, and learning. Now it's your turn to answer those questions.

TUNING IN TO YOURSELF

What matters most right now?

The best way to answer this question is simply to write down the first two or three things that come into your mind. If it's difficult to think of something, you can reference a wellness wheel, which is something I do with clients who have a hard time finding answers. Of the sections in the wheel, which three matter most to you right now?

continued

1. Physical
2. Mental
3. Emotional
4. Spiritual
5. Financial
6. Vocational
7. Environmental
8. Social

Notice that I added the words *right now* to this question. As we move through life, we change and our circumstances change. That means our passions and priorities change, and what matters most evolves.

What is valuable to you?
Really push yourself to dig deeper with this question. Aim for a list of eight to ten things, then rank and prioritize them. Keep in mind all the messaging that gets put on you daily about what you should value. Set all that aside and get out of your head. Listen to your heart. Putting your hand on your heart while asking this question can help you tune in.

Look at your answers. What surprises you about them? What new things did you learn?

APPLYING WHAT'S MEANINGFUL AND VALUABLE

Starting my business forced me into what felt like a crash course in what was meaningful and valuable to me. As any entrepreneur can attest to, you feel like there is never enough time in the day to get to everything, let alone get everything done. Once you get the business off the ground, you are forced to face these questions or you will be so overwhelmed that you fail or plateau and have a hard time growing. The questions of what's meaningful and valuable can be powerful to consider not only in your life but also in your work, because most people have different answers. If you want, pause here and consider how you'd answer these questions related to work.

I learned that what matters most to me in the work I get to do—what is meaningful—is the chance to dream with people about what's possible as they consider their future and to help them see potential in themselves so they can build their confidence. As my business grew, I encountered a lot of operational and administrative tasks that had to be done to make a profit, work effectively, and provide a good experience, but I didn't want to spend my time on them. I had to hire someone to do those things, so I could stay focused on what was meaningful and valuable to me, what I am called to and uniquely gifted to do.

Connection also matters to me. Quality means more than quantity to me. This is a huge shift that I am still working to make. For a long time, I went to all the events and tried to know as many people as possible. At this stage, I really value connecting with people who want to go beyond the surface level, and I'm working to proactively put my time and energy into experiences that allow for that.

As my business has grown, I have realized that I value clients who align with the business's core values, which are an extension of my own, and who are committed to doing their work more than I value clients who pay well. These lessons have come from working with clients who could pay but weren't committed, and those who received a financial concession from me and flourished and had life-changing results.

The last thing I'll share to keep those wheels turning is that I value having more time. The work that I do with individuals and organizations goes deep and requires a lot of focus and attention. It is so different from the work I did in the corporate world. Much of the work I did in my sales career was transactional—based on numbers, results, and getting things done. As I matured and moved into leadership roles, the work became more relational, more about building trust and alignment and helping and serving others. Now I see the value in moving to the next level, which is moving from transactional to relational and finally to transformational. No matter *what* we do for a job, we have the opportunity to do it in one of these three ways, but each requires a different approach. Connection and care are so much deeper when we move into the transactional realm, and this requires more time and energy. As I have moved into doing my work from a transformational place, I have come to realize that the value of my work goes down if I don't leave enough space in the day to process my time and ideas with my clients. As someone who was pretty addicted to getting things done, I have come to value my downtime and white space—my time to invest in care; to process, think, and discern; to reset and regroup; to pray; and so on. That's where things come together, ideas crystallize, and the real magic of my work takes place.

NAVIGATING DIFFERENCES OF OPINION ABOUT WHAT'S MEANINGFUL AND VALUABLE

One of the most common polarities in what's meaningful and valuable is when one person values comfort, contentment, and security, and someone else values growth, change, and risk. This difference can cause conflict or misunderstanding between people in any relationship, whether family, work, or community. I have the privilege of working with several teenage clients, and this is often a source of tension within a family. Generational dynamics and life experiences have conditioned each group of parents and children to have certain views about life and work—and different sets of values.

While this example is a generalization, I'm offering it for a better understanding of how these differences can form within a family. For instance, in a family where the parents have done so well to provide stability and security, I find kids are much more comfortable with allowing things to be as they are and simply enjoying life. The parents are inclined to push for growth, and the kids have become wired for comfort. The parents may perceive the kids as "lazy" or "unmotivated," and the kids may perceive their parents as "overbearing" or "unrealistic." Consider how this dynamic plays out more broadly in our society and how our familial experiences have changed over time.

For parents in their forties and fifties, as of the time this book is being published, they watched the generations before them work hard and sacrifice a lot to provide financial security. They heard stories of and even witnessed the family going from poor and struggling to more stable and secure. They learned that hard work and sacrifice of family and extracurricular time is what is required to get and keep security. I am oversimplifying this narrative by leaving out the way that the employer–employee relationship has changed and how cultural dynamics overall have evolved so as not to make this chapter a book in and of itself, but do you see how this has created certain beliefs and perceptions about life and work—and, more broadly, an ideal of the "right way" to live? I encourage you to reflect more holistically on your own family story, so you can pick up on how the history and experiences in your family created stories, perceptions, and beliefs that shape what you feel matters today.

Think about what happens as more and more generations are removed from the stories and experiences of their grandparents and great-grandparents. Most of the young people I work with have really only known a life of security, stability, and having more than enough from a material standpoint. This creates a new narrative and relationship with work that is very different from the one their parents have. It also creates a different narrative about life and community. These narratives create a different set of values. For example, one of my young people said she wanted to be a teacher, but her dad continued to push her to get into school administration so she could earn more money. He values money over the job itself while she sees that if she were to move into administration, she would not be able to work closely with the students, which is what she knows she would love to do.

Another student, when I asked her to rank what was most important to her between friends, grades, and sports, shared with me that friends (relationships) were most important to her, but she knew that her parents would not like that answer. She felt pressured to put school above everything, so she could get good grades to go to a good college and get a high-paying job. She was able to recognize that she watched her parents sacrifice a lot of their personal life and relationships in the pursuit of money, and she didn't want to do the same thing. She felt like that choice would leave her stressed out and lonely. Each of us has different ideas about what's meaningful and valuable to us.

INFLUENCE OF PEOPLE AND CULTURE ON WHAT WE BELIEVE IS MEANINGFUL AND VALUABLE

In thinking about our differences in what we believe to be meaningful and valuable, let's look at another dynamic: the impact of culture and the people we surround ourselves with. Most of us are completely unaware of how the environment around us and the people we surround ourselves with impact us. We see messages that influence how we think about what's meaningful and valuable all around us on billboards, TV shows, the radio, and social media. Everywhere we look, we are being sold and told something. We already discussed the importance of becoming more aware and controlling what we take in. We also need to consider the people we surround ourselves with.

I'm not suggesting that we compound the issue we already have in our society by only aligning ourselves to and spending time with people who are like us. That does more harm. What I am suggesting is taking an inventory of the people we are around the most. In what areas are we aligned, and in what ways are we different? Humans are complex, and being in relationships is complicated. It's easy to say we like or dislike someone in a broad stroke without realizing our ignorance. Let's break down some of our closest relationships.

EVALUATING YOUR RELATIONSHIPS

List the five people you spend the most time with.
Be sure to list the ones you actually do spend the most time with, rather than those you want to spend time with. People from family and work will likely top the list for most.

Take each person you listed and jot down three things you have in common and three things you don't.
You are not making this list out of judgment, and it doesn't need to be shared. This is for your own growth, so write what comes to your heart and mind.

UNDERSTANDING AND LEVERAGING THE INFLUENCES OF OTHERS

Look at what you've written about your relationships. This exercise is meant to help you realize where you need to be mindful of a person's influence on what's meaningful and valuable to you and how you might need to adapt or adjust to ensure you can stay in your integrity and honor the other person while maintaining your relationship. For me, this often points out where I can trust the judgment of the other person or where I may need to push a little. It is a guide to help me establish standards and boundaries in relationships and understand how and where to ask for input and feedback.

For example, my husband is more deliberate and risk-averse than I am. When it comes to large purchases or suggestions for where we stay on vacation, I always go along with his recommendation because I know we are aligned from a cost and quality perspective, and I can be sure he has done the research to find the option that will suit us best. When it comes to initiating a conversation about going on a vacation and deciding where we could go, I leverage my skills and abilities to dream up options and make sure we actually go on a vacation. See how that works?

In another example, my business partner and I share the same values and vision for our practice but differ on our comfort level related to what's possible, timing, and sacrifices made. We honor that in each other. I'm going to push us, and she's going to pull us. This typically helps us get to the right spot. I'll dream up a dream, she'll say not now, I'll push for details on when, and we'll continue leaning in until we get to something that we both feel comfortable and confident in.

If you have to spend time with people you are more misaligned with, it will be challenging, so it will be important to point out to yourself and keep in mind where you *are* aligned. Just bringing these realities to our conscious awareness helps us be less frustrated and allows us to choose whether we let that frustration stay with us or seep into other areas of our lives. We can always find common ground, and we get to choose whether we allow ourselves to focus on where we are aligned or misaligned.

In going through this exercise, one of my clients had a hard time naming any ways that he was aligned with his boss. Their personalities were different, they valued different things, their styles for leadership were different, and they didn't agree on priorities. They were in constant conflict. He liked his job, but this relationship with his boss was making things very difficult, and the stress was bleeding into his personal life in ways he didn't like. We talked through his options. He started to put some boundaries in place and began to be more open about the ways they were misaligned. In doing so, it became clear that his boss was unwilling to listen to his perspective or consider doing anything different. He was now faced with a tough decision: learn how to adapt to this new reality and find ways to minimize the impact on him and his life, or go find another job.

There is no right or wrong answer in these situations. It comes back to you and what consequences you are willing to deal with because it's your life. Some of the trickiest situations are when you are misaligned with members of your own family. You have to choose whether and how to stay in a relationship with them or not. There are real consequences to both choices.

Now let's talk about the fun and positive part of being impacted by the people we are around. I want to give you an opportunity to consider who you respect and admire most in your life. Who do you want to be more like? How can you spend more time with these people? If you're anything like me, my schedule gets filled with activities or people asking me to do things, and I don't always get time with the people I'd most like to spend time with. Let's change that! It starts with identifying those people, then making a plan for when and how you can spend more time with them. Even if you have a busy schedule, purposefully and proactively choosing who you call, text, email, send a thank-you note to, or grab coffee or lunch with can be small ways to be more in touch with people who will positively impact your life.

POSITIVE IMPACTS THROUGH YOUR RELATIONSHIPS

List the five people you admire most in your life who you'd like to spend more time with.
What is preventing you from spending time with them? It could be distance, it could be that you are in different seasons of life so schedules don't align, or it could be that you perceive them to be busy and don't want to be a burden by asking them to spend time with you.

List some ways that you could be in contact with each person you listed and get more time with them.
Depending on where your relationship currently sits, you could start with sending handwritten notes or texts, and as your relationship grows, move into more in-person visits or activities.

BECOMING INTENTIONAL ABOUT WHO YOU SPEND TIME WITH

There will be people in your life who want to spend time with you but who you aren't particularly thrilled about spending time with. The same might be true for the people you are reaching out to. You may not be on their list. That's OK. Trust that as you work through this process, you will get to spend more time with the people who are more aligned with you. Relationships are tricky and rarely mutual moment to moment, but over time, you can work to spend time with those people who give and receive in the relationship, and who are more aligned than misaligned with who and where you are.

As life changes, these relationships change because we change as individuals. There may be times when a friend needs you and you are giving more than receiving in the relationship. Be mindful of this, and be sure that you are spending time with them when you have something to give, not when you're depleted. At the same time, consider who can give you what you need in a relationship, so you don't end up spending time with people who are only taking from you. As you change, allow your relationships to change and the amount of time you spend with people to change. This is a natural part of life and doesn't mean we love anyone more or less. Others may not like it when you start to create distance, but if you are honoring your heart and your needs, you do what's best for all parties.

A friend I hadn't seen or talked with in a few months recently reached out. I agreed to meet with him, but it just wasn't sitting right in my heart. As I sat with how I was really feeling and what I was honestly thinking without judging myself, I realized I felt more obligated to meet with him than motivated to. I reflected on our relationship and our last few interactions and realized why. He typically reaches out to me when he needs something. During our time together, he spends most of it sharing his issues and asking for advice. He rarely reaches out to see how I'm doing, and he hasn't been supportive of my business or community efforts in ways that are meaningful to me. The relationship has developed into something very one-sided.

This realization, along with the recognition of where I was and what I needed at that time, empowered me to text him back and let him know I would not be able to get together at this time. I felt a huge weight lift. Later that day during my prayer time, a message came to me loud and clear that really helped me: By saying no to him, I was allowing someone who really wanted to support him and spend time with him to say yes. It would have been selfish of me to spend that time knowing I didn't really want to be there and my heart wasn't in it. Can you relate?

I want to point out that this is not meant to be an exercise of selfishness but awareness. We want to serve others and be there for them in their times of need, just as we would want others to do for us. We must recognize in ourselves what we need, what we have to give, and what the person is asking of us, and engage in a way that honors ourselves and the other person, not in a way that is half-hearted and violates either person. This may cause conflict and stress in relationships, and that is OK. Being in a relationship is messy, especially as we navigate our individual perspectives, desires, and needs.

Being in relationships with others is part of what makes finding out what is meaningful and valuable to us so difficult. When we add in the influences and people in our lives and how they can impact those narratives and experiences, things get complicated. We are told from a young age that there is one right away to live. In a world filled with endless options and information, we have the freedom to explore and the responsibility to listen to our hearts as we do it, so we find the path that fits us best.

EVALUATING HOW WE SPEND OUR RESOURCES AGAINST WHAT'S MEANINGFUL AND VALUABLE

Hopefully, through our journey in this chapter so far, you have become more aware of what's meaningful and valuable to those around you and how that has impacted your perspectives and beliefs around what's meaningful and valuable to you. At the end of the day, each of us has a different picture of what is meaningful and valuable, and what we are comfortable sacrificing and what we are not. We alone have to live with the consequences of our choices. When we reconnect with our truth about what's meaningful and valuable, then we need to consider how we may need to change how we are investing our time, money, and energy to keep those things a priority.

Now, take a moment and bring what's meaningful and valuable to you back to the front of your mind and consider where you spend your time, energy, and money. (If you need to go back to those two questions and dig for deeper and truer answers, I encourage you to do that now.) The first time people get clear on what's meaningful and valuable, they usually discover quite a gap between what they have in their hearts, what's happening in their daily lives, and what's prioritized in their schedules. The next couple of exercises will help close that gap.

Before we start, keep in mind there will always be areas where we are out of alignment with how we prioritize our time, energy, and money around what's meaningful and valuable to us. We have good intentions, and then life happens. In the following sections, we will look at what is aligned and what isn't—and intentionally start with what is aligned, because I want you to feel good and celebrate where you are. Think about how far you've come to get to this point and remind yourself that you are a work in progress. This is a never-ending recalibration, and we need to celebrate progress every chance we get!

As you realize what is out of alignment, give yourself grace. Be reasonable and realistic about what you can and want to do about it. Keep in mind that we all go through seasons too. We are looking at the big, overall picture. If you are in a busy season at work or something significant just occurred in your life, then you may be more misaligned than normal and stay that way for a while. If that's you, please don't feel pressure to make big adjustments now. Just know when those realignments will be coming, and recognize that may be a reason you aren't feeling great about things right now.

YOUR TIME, ENERGY, AND MONEY

- List the top five things that take up your time right now.
- List the top five things that take up your energy right now.
- List the top five things you spend your money on right now.

If you have a hard time going this broad, imagine a typical day, week, or month. You could even go back and audit your calendar or planner for help. Remember, you are a whole person, so you are looking at the whole of your life—personal, professional, and everything in between. What does this picture tell you?

How do these answers match up, or not, with what's meaningful and valuable to you? Or in other words, where are you aligned and where do you need to make adjustments?

TAKING TIME TO EXPLORE AND UNDERSTAND OUR MISALIGNMENTS

Before we jump into what we will do to become more aligned, let's explore what you have found in the last exercise about how you spend your time, money, and energy. Going deeper—making time to think, not just to be aware—is where the learning happens and where you will integrate insights that will keep you learning long after you put this book down. We all operate on autopilot in certain areas that may have gotten out of whack because a season turned into a permanent change or because a pattern or habit got deeply ingrained into our daily routine without us realizing it. Challenge yourself to slow down and not skip from identifying an issue to solving it. Give yourself space to make a closer examination and expand your exploration. This helps you identify things that will prevent misalignments from happening again in the number or depth at which they are happening today.

The following list includes some of the most common misalignments I've seen through my practice. I share these so you know you are not alone and to bring awareness to some things you may have overlooked or not considered yet. These are narratives I hear over and over coming out of this exercise.

1. My family is the most valuable to me, but they get the least amount of time and energy.

2. Time at home is meaningful and valuable to me, but I have filled my schedule, so I never get it.

3. Time alone is valuable to me but rarely happens.

4. Friends are important to me, but I see or speak with them very rarely.

5. My faith is important to me, but I'm only spending time with God in church on Sundays.

6. Quiet time is something I crave, but I can't find time in my schedule for it.

7. I spend a lot of time watching TV or scrolling through my phone.

8. Eating healthy is important to me, but I don't make time for meal prep or planning ahead.

9. Working out and a focus on my fitness would make me feel better, but I don't make it a priority.

10. I love to learn and read but can't seem to find the time to do it.

11. Saving money is important, but I've made financial choices that don't leave much to save.

12. I spend a lot of money on things that I don't need, use, or wear.

13. A lot of my energy is spent trying to control things I have no control over.

14. I'm so worried about the future or so wrapped up in the past that I'm missing the present.

15. I'm working in a job I don't like because I feel like I have to for the financial gain or because of expectations I put on myself or that others have of me.

Do any of these resonate with you? Or did other misalignments come to mind? Add them to the list you've already compiled.

Now, spend some time breaking them down to deepen your understanding of them. What surprised you the most? What were you completely unaware of until this exercise? How did these things come to be?

By examining the root cause and being honest about what surprised you, you can start to make internal, transformational shifts. You are moving from awareness to understanding, and this evolution in your consciousness and knowledge helps shift patterns and habits in ways that will keep you more aligned in the future. You will notice these things earlier and make the necessary adjustments to stay aligned to what's meaningful and valuable to you.

MOVING INTO ALIGNMENT

What is one thing you can do to become more aligned?
Look at the list you compiled in the previous exercise and choose the one misalignment that is most important to you. Yes, you are going to start with practicing, implementing, and integrating one. Remember, mastery happens with small, focused

effort. You want to get something integrated before you try and make the next adjustment.

As you move toward creating more alignment, it's important to believe that your efforts to make this change are worth it and any sacrifices you need to make to get more into alignment will be good for you in the long run. Building a vision for what could be connects you to what's possible and motivates you to move forward. Now, explore your misalignment by asking these questions:

- What will it look and feel like to be fully aligned in this area?
- What would be different if you were aligned in this area?
- What impacts would it have on you and those around you?

Before you take action, you also want to consider the practical and tactical steps you need to take and what might get in your way. By preparing in this way, your heart and mind are better equipped to stay committed when you meet resistance or encounter surprises in the process. Ask yourself the following:

- What do you need to start or stop doing?
- What are the milestones (outcomes you will see or changes you will make)? By when?
- Who can you lean on for support?
- What happens if you backslide?

Many of my clients put what's meaningful and valuable to them and their list of people they wish to spend more time with on paper and keep it somewhere visible to serve as a reminder while they are making decisions. When these things are not top of mind as choices are brought to us, it's easy to revert to old patterns and habits.

Another great practice is to simply visit your list and do your time, energy, and money audit once a week, once a month, or once a quarter to continue to move yourself toward further alignment. It's important to do whatever is best for you, given that you have one precious life to live. Make it matter and make it meaningful.

REALIGNING WHAT'S MEANINGFUL AND VALUABLE IN OUR LEADERSHIP

You have likely gone through the exercises so far looking at and answering the questions through a personal lens. Now let's change our glasses and answer them from a professional lens. Just like every human is different, every leader is different. When we are fully integrated people, operating mostly the same at work as we do at home, much of what we find meaningful and valuable in life will be the same. But there can be circumstantial differences, depending on how we view work and what assumptions we have about people's expectations of us. For example, if you believe that at work you are expected to be extroverted to be successful in your role but you are naturally introverted, then you may find different things more meaningful and valuable in your professional life than in your personal life. Another example is authenticity and transparency. Some people who find these two things meaningful and valuable in their personal life struggle to understand how and what to share at work without doing harm or sharing too much.

Most of us would say that who we are at work is the more "cleaned up and polished" version of ourselves. We are more thoughtful about what we say and how we act. Just like our family stories and experiences shape what's meaningful and valuable to us, often without our awareness, the environment, expectations, norms, and values of an organization can shape what is meaningful and valuable to us in our leadership without our awareness. Let's bring all the preceding questions into this conversation, and answer them through the lens of work and leadership. If you find yourself thinking and acting in a fundamentally different way in your personal life than in your professional life, these questions will be even more important to explore.

TUNING IN TO YOURSELF AS A LEADER

What matters most right now?
Write down the first two or three things that come to your mind. If you have a hard time doing that, refer back to the wellness wheel I mentioned earlier. Of the sections, which three matter most to you right now?

1.	Physical	5.	Financial
2.	Mental	6.	Vocational
3.	Emotional	7.	Environmental
4.	Spiritual	8.	Social

What is valuable to you?
Write down the first things that come to mind. Give yourself a bit more time to think and add anything else that comes up.

When it comes to answering these questions for work and leadership, I often find clients hesitant to be honest. They want to give a moral or more desirable answer when the truth is, for example, that money matters most. Denying your truth and the reality of how you feel will keep you from getting any benefit from this exercise. There is no shame or judgment here. If we aren't honest about where we are, we can't get to where we want to be. If any of your answers cause you to hesitate or think twice, give yourself some time to consider why that might be. There are lessons and insights there waiting for you. When you're ready, let's move to the people you spend the most time with at work and those you'd like to spend more time with.

YOUR PROFESSIONAL RELATIONSHIPS

List the five people you spend the most time with at work.
Now take each one and walk through three things you have in common and three things you don't. Remember, be honest.

How have these people impacted your behavior at work and brought you into or out of alignment with what's meaningful and valuable to you? What does this tell you about how you may need to adjust your approach or boundaries or be more mindful of the ways they impact you?

List the five people you admire most in your professional life that you'd like to spend more time with.
Why do you want to spend more time with them? What are three things you admire about them? In what ways do you aspire to be more like them? How can they bring you more into alignment about what's meaningful and valuable to you?

What are a couple of ways you could be in more contact with each person listed?

WEIGHING THE MISALIGNMENTS YOU EXPERIENCE AT WORK

What have you learned so far about what's meaningful and valuable to you in leadership and how those around you impact you? Keep these things in mind as we move into our time, energy, and money audit. Within the hierarchical structure of most workplaces, authority is given to certain people to make decisions, and these decisions directly impact us, especially when it comes to where we spend our time, money, and energy.

If you recognize major misalignments with people you have to work closely with, there will likely be misalignments related to what's meaningful and valuable to you and where you are spending your time, money, and energy. Instead of placing blame or playing victim, I challenge you to consider what role you can fill to influence these decisions now that you know what you know.

Who can be an ally, confidant, or advocate for you? What are your deal-breakers or nonnegotiables related to these misalignments? I have worked for leaders with whom I was aligned and with whom I was not. I have worked inside organizations where most of the people I worked with mostly aligned with what I thought was meaningful and valuable, and I have had the opposite experience. The reality is that if there are major misalignments at an individual or collective level, we will expend energy resisting what we are asked to do, or we will experience stress from being out of alignment with ourselves.

These are complex scenarios, and it's important that we identify the weight of the misalignments, the stress, and energetic trade-offs caused by them, and it's important that we understand our nonnegotiables. For instance, you may disagree with your leader on how a project is to be executed, and even if that misalignment continues to surface, you can work through it because the weight of that issue is fairly insignificant. On the other hand, if you disagree with the way your company thinks about client service and provides service, or the way your boss thinks about employees and treats them, the weight of these misalignments may offer you a chance to consider if you're in the right workplace.

YOUR TIME, ENERGY, AND MONEY AT WORK

In light of the discussion on workplace misalignments, take some time to explore the following:

- List the top five things that take up your time right now.
- List the top five things that take up your energy right now.
- List the top five things you spend your money on right now.
- What does this picture tell you?
- What are the misalignments between where you're spending your time, energy, and money and what's meaningful and valuable to you?
- What do you have control over? What don't you have control over?
- What trade-offs or decisions do these realities force you to face?

THE IMPORTANCE OF ONGOING REEVALUATION AND REALIGNMENT

The best leaders know they will be reflecting and realigning almost constantly because of the pace of change—culture change, industry change, technology change, legal and economic changes, organizational change, and individual change. When things continue to change, we need to continue to make time and space for reevaluation and realignment.

What we once thought was best may no longer be. The trade-offs and decisions we are forced to face are the primary reason we don't like to do this exercise. Maybe we have put work in front of our relationships. Maybe a position or even the entire organization has outgrown us or someone on the team. Maybe what we used to recognize and reward should change based on where we are and what phase we're in . . . and we're just too busy to think it all through.

These small misalignments, when left unaddressed, pile up and have significant impacts on our leadership and team effectiveness. As a culture, we don't value the idea of stepping back, slowing down, and getting things right. The more work we put into being thoughtful about creating our vision for what's meaningful and valuable and aligning our daily thoughts, habits, and behaviors to it, the easier our life gets. This is a simple truth that we forget because culture tells us to just keep *doing*, and reinforces that *thinking* is unproductive and a waste of time.

Think of it like a balloon. If we squeeze the front end, which symbolizes jumping straight from idea to action, not spending time thinking through implications and impacts, not reflecting and realigning, then all the air in the balloon goes to the back, representing all the confusion, frustration, and issues we have to deal with later. When we have the courage to push all of that time and energy to the front end, then we lessen the frustration, confusion, and issues on the back end.

BUILDING SELF-TRUST BY ALIGNING OUR INTENTIONS AND ACTIONS

Another issue we face if we don't slow down and give ourselves time to reflect and realign is that we degrade trust. We are blind to how our intentions and actions are misaligned, and we send mixed messages in our words and behavior. I regularly see several common misalignments like this with my clients:

- I say I value my people, but I don't hold one-on-ones or consistently cancel them.

- I say that values matter as much as performance, but I recognize and reward the high-performing salesperson, even though she regularly displays behavior that goes against our values or even hurts others.

- I say I value a mature and disciplined approach to leadership, but I consistently show up unprepared.

- I say inclusivity and collaboration are important, but I consistently make decisions without including other people in the process.

- I say that being open-minded and having a growth mindset are valued, but I consistently shut people and ideas down that aren't in line with my way of thinking.

To get and keep the trust of others, we have to trust ourselves. If I ask people whether they trust themselves, they usually say yes. As I probe deeper, and if they are willing to be honest, I often experience them coming around to a no. We are so focused on whether we trust others that we don't make time to think about what it would look or feel like if we trusted ourselves.

There are two areas where I see clients discover that they may need to work on rebuilding trust with themselves: 1) the commitments they've made to themselves and 2) their relationships. As I ask clients about how they have delivered on the commitments they've made to themselves, we uncover a gap between intention and action. We set goals and make commitments, but our actions don't change, or we don't follow through and are quickly out of our integrity with ourselves. We have broken our own trust.

To build and maintain our self-trust, we have to be clear about our intent. What do we want? Why do we want it? Are we willing to do what it takes, even make difficult sacrifices, to get it? When we develop goals and commitments, time and time again, we make them because of other people. We see others pursuing something—losing weight, running a half-marathon, reading more books, you name it—and we think, "I should do that too."

When we make goals and commitments in this way, we haven't done the deep work to develop the resolve to stick to them. First, we need to give ourselves space to really think about why we desire a certain goal. How will this change me? What will be different on the other side? What sacrifices will I need to make? What are the steps to get there? We have to develop a path to stay in our integrity as we walk this out because it's likely going to butt up against what we have been thinking, believing, or doing for some time.

When we take more time to think through our goals and commitments, we will be better able to match our intentions and actions and stay in our integrity. We will recognize ourselves delivering on our commitments instead of defying or denying ourselves, and this will continue to build self-trust and confidence. As this grows inside of us, our ability to trust others will grow. We have to trust ourselves in order to trust others.

BUILDING SELF-TRUST BY HONORING OURSELVES AND OUR INTUITION IN RELATIONSHIPS

When it comes to losing self-trust because of relationships, clients commonly share their habit of overriding their intuition and being let down. Each of us has a gut feeling about someone when we first meet them. I do not want to encourage that we shut people out because of that gut feeling (because many of us are so far disconnected from our intuition, we need to relearn how to use it), but to build and maintain trust with ourselves, we need to practice using our intuition again by acknowledging those gut feelings, listening to what they are telling us, and exploring where it's all coming from.

Make space for thinking and feeling your way through this. Think of a recent interaction with someone where you had a strong gut feeling, positive or negative. What is that feeling? What could the feeling be signaling to you? Sometimes, we are triggered by someone because of something that happened to us in the past. It has nothing to do with that person. Some of us are triggered by physical similarities, tone of voice, things people say, a certain energy someone brings. We often refer to this as *unconscious bias*.

We need to make space for discernment, so we can pull these narratives apart and peel the bias back. To stay in your integrity in a relationship of any kind, this bias must be explored. If you find yourself drawn to or repelled by someone, but determine it has nothing to do with that actual individual, you have identified an area you may need to explore or heal from. If it persists with regard to that specific person, then you need to consider how you can best be in a relationship with them.

For instance, how much time should you spend with and how much access should you give this person? What do you need to do to make this relationship work? When we don't listen to our intuition and consider these questions, we end up in situations where we are denying and defying our instincts, which breaks our self-trust. When we acknowledge the challenge and set up boundaries and parameters in the relationship, we honor ourselves and the other person, and we prevent a negative experience in the relationship.

THE IMPACT OF OUR PERSONAL EXPERIENCES ON OUR PROFESSIONAL RELATIONSHIPS

My professional relationships have been impacted by my personal experiences. I have been in personal relationships with several men who exerted power over me or took advantage of me, including some who were abusive. When I found myself working with a man, be it my direct boss or boss's boss, who I didn't feel listened to me or cared about my perspective, I became triggered. I found myself bringing protective and negative energy into meetings with that person, arguing with what they had to say, and resisting any ideas or orders, even if I agreed with them.

A client of mine realized after a few coaching sessions that she was triggered daily because she reported to someone who rarely, if ever, validated her ideas or gave her feedback that she was on the right track, and sometimes even took credit for her ideas and work. Now, this situation would likely bother anyone, but the intensity of the emotions she was feeling and the reaction she had indicated to me that there was something more going on. After some reflection and exploring, she realized that her mother had done the same thing to her as she was growing up. She'd felt like she was never good enough and was trying to fill that need and void she felt from her relationship with her mother in this work relationship.

In these situations, we don't necessarily have the power to limit our interaction with the person, but we do have the power to shift our own perspectives, change our expectations, and set boundaries for ourselves. We can think about what we need to do to create a healthy environment for this professional relationship and what we may need to stay in good standing within the relationship—less one-on-one time with the person, more time to process, or time to come back to neutral mentally and emotionally after an interaction (versus being in a heightened emotional state or telling ourselves stories that aren't true and are projected on this situation based on our past experiences).

There are instances when we just can't put our finger on why we don't mesh with someone. It's simply a feeling in our gut that won't go away. We can honor that too and consider what is within our control to make the relationship work. While some people may encourage that we cut a relationship off altogether, unless there is outright abuse, I would suggest that every person and relationship is an opportunity to refine our skills and our spirit and to grow. You may need to take a break from someone for a period of time to regroup and come back in.

Being in relationships with others is complex. We all bring different ideas, assumptions, and expectations to our relationships, many of them left unsaid. We see potential in someone and create expectations around that potential without speaking those expectations out loud. We make assumptions about a relationship based on our past experiences and, again, never say them out loud. This sets us up for failure.

Bring to your awareness how you feel about someone. Be honest about where that comes from: Is it them or is it you? Focus on what you can do to change yourself or the situation. When we spend time on what the other person needs to change, we waste our precious time and energy because we simply have no control over that. Putting in the work to create healthy relationships is challenging but worth every ounce of effort. We need each other, and life's more enjoyable when we are connected.

We covered a lot of ground in this chapter to help you understand what's meaningful and valuable to you. If self-trust and relationships aren't on your list, you may want to reconsider adding these foundational elements of living a meaningful and intentional life to it. Trusting ourselves is incredibly important because what's meaningful and valuable to you may not be meaningful and valuable to someone else. You have to reconnect with yourself, your intuition, and your intention, remaining rooted in your identity before you can move to the next step and envision what's possible.

REFLECT ON YOUR JOURNEY

- What have you learned, unlearned, or relearned in this chapter?
- What has been most valuable to you?
- What one thing will you commit to doing differently going forward?
- Who can you invite in to keep you accountable?

CHAPTER 9

Envisioning What's Possible

To this point in our journey together, we have created understanding, cleared away what isn't ours, and done some work to rebuild our self-trust and gain a deeper understanding of what's truly meaningful and valuable to us. Now is the most fun part of the journey . . . well, to me, the dreamer, it is . . . and I hope you will enjoy it too. We get to spend time thinking and dreaming about who you are at your best.

Keeping in mind all that you have learned and uncovered to this point, let's wade into this work. We will explore your passions and gifts, your definition of success, and what your life and leadership could look like without any constraints, and I will also challenge you to consider the end of your life and what will matter most to you then.

Many of us avoid thinking about our own mortality because we're scared of death, but when we do, things become a lot clearer. What matters most has a way of coming to the surface, and the rest of the noise and distractions fall away. I invite you to go through the questions in the exercises in this chapter with little input from anyone else. Allow yourself to really listen to your heart and tap into your vision and desires. The next step will be to ask for input from others, so give yourself this chance to really look inside yourself and explore.

We will begin this envisioning process by exploring your passions and your unique gifts. Our passions indicate things we should pay attention to. These are things we deeply desire, things that drive us and make us feel alive, and causes we care about. They are typically developed through our life experiences and are so ingrained in who we are that we are surprised when others aren't as passionate about them as we are. Let's dig into what your personal passions are.

YOUR PASSIONS

Take some time to think about and write down your responses to these questions:

- What do you desire?
- What drives you?
- What makes you feel alive?
- What causes do you care about?
- What other passions come to mind for you?

UNCOVERING YOUR PASSIONS

How did that feel? How are you feeling now? Exploring your passions is an important exercise because it can give you renewed energy and hope for the future. It's easy to fall into the mundane routines and comfort of everyday life and disconnect from what we are doing it all for in the first place. When we are feeling depleted or even defeated, this is a good exercise to come back to.

Review your answers. Is there anything you left out because you thought it was obvious? Write that down. If it lights a fire in you, even if it's something simple, put it on paper. Sometimes those things that are the most obvious to us are easy to overlook, when in reality, they are exactly where we should be putting our energy.

For example, I am passionate about self-discovery and challenging myself to grow. I assumed for a long time that these were also passions for every person because they were so deeply ingrained in who I am. On vacation I was always drawn to making space for a good book or two that would stretch my mind and soul. Not a casual book, but something deep, meaningful, or even hard. Friends we traveled with questioned why I would want to read that kind of book on vacation. I found that kind of reading refreshing, while others found it exhausting.

A friend of mine loves gardening. He loves the feeling of his hands in the dirt. He enjoys the process of preparing the ground and the seeds, tending to them and pulling weeds, and witnessing things grow. There are a million reasons he's passionate about gardening, but it's not a passion area for me. How about you? What insights are available to you now that you've more intentionally explored your passions?

EXPLORING YOUR UNIQUE GIFTS

Like your passions, your gifts are something that are such an integral part of who you are, you probably don't realize they are gifts. Your gifts are the things you are known for, that come naturally to you, and that make you feel energized. I have a client who is so good at thinking up new ideas that he didn't realize this was difficult for other people. His gift is ideation. Give him a challenge and he can come up with a thousand ideas of how to overcome it.

I have a friend who lights up a room and makes everyone feel warm and welcome wherever she goes. This is her gift. Consider what people compliment you for regularly. And consider that many of our gifts have more to do with *who* we are and *how* we are, than what we do.

YOUR GIFTS

Now, let's explore what your gifts are. Take some time to think about and write down your responses to the following questions:

- What are you known for?
- What do people regularly compliment you for?
- What are your strengths?
- What comes naturally to you?
- What gives you energy?

What did you discover about your gifts? What does this tell you about where you should spend your time and energy? How does this impact your view of yourself, your life, and your work? If we are living our lives in a way that hinders our ability to use our gifts, we are limiting our contributions to the world. We may also be depleting ourselves of energy.

Helping clients uncover or rediscover their gifts is one of the greatest joys of my coaching career. When people experience that *aha* moment and recognize that they have unique gifts that can be used for good, they are forever transformed. It's fun to witness people as they see their lives and daily experiences through new eyes, and as they find ways to apply their gifts in different ways. Now take a moment. Look at your lists of passions and gifts and consider what else you could do with your life and work. How could you better leverage these for good in the world in a way that lights you up and makes you feel alive?

I have come to realize in my own life and work that my ability to connect with others and make them feel safe and seen is a unique gift. People share things with me they've never shared with someone else. Strangers often say to me, "I don't know why I'm telling you this." I love it. Before I realized it was a gift, I took it for granted and left it mostly unused in my daily life. I was so focused on getting things done that I wasn't leaving space for these connections with others. Now that I have fully accepted this gift, I leave more margin in my days and allow these meaningful moments to happen more frequently. This gift has changed my life, and people I've shared it with have told me that it has changed theirs. That's the power of living our gifts.

REDISCOVERING YOUR DREAMS

Next, let's move deeper into your heart. There are longings and dreams that we have made quiet or given up on. We often abandon these dreams because someone tells us that pursuing them is a waste of time or that we will never make them a reality. We also do it because we get busy or life gets in the way. Some of us abandon these dreams and desires because keeping them alive while we live out the realities of where we are in life is too painful.

If this is you, I want to encourage you to go there anyway. Allow those dreams and desires to resurface. There is nothing you need to do with them. You don't have to act on them in any way, but it is important that you honor them. You can release them with a valid reason and purposefully allow them to lie dormant versus avoiding or ignoring them. My ultimate hope is that you rediscover or remember something that wakes up your soul in a new way and reignites your passion for life and work, even if you are in a season where you can't act on those dreams or desires today.

One of the main reasons we abandon our dreams is because we are afraid to fail. Even deeper, we are afraid of how successful we might be. Allowing ourselves to dream means we have to be ready to walk into the unknown, and most of us don't like the unknown. This is another issue rooted in a lack of self-trust.

If you recall, we previously talked about how we can build or break self-trust through acting with or against our intent and integrity. This has to do with our character. We also build or break self-trust through capability, our ability to do things well, and results or the outcomes we experience. This has to do with our competence. So many of us are afraid to fail. It is one of the top fears that hold us back from reaching our potential. But we can't get results and make progress if we aren't willing to risk failure. When something is new or unknown, we have to at least have the courage to fail. It doesn't mean we will, but we have to be willing to wade into the possibility of failure. It's just the nature of new things. We can't always be good at something we just started. We have to meet ourselves where we are and allow ourselves to learn and grow.

THE DESIRE FOR COMPETENCE AND THE INHERENT RISK OF FAILURE

Acknowledging and accepting failure has taken me years and years to remember and relearn . . . and I still struggle. In the past, if I wasn't good at something, I would just quit. Many would argue that quitting is OK because you should be focused on your strengths. My marriage and my business are just two of several examples that fly in the face of that idea. I was not a naturally good partner in marriage. The beginning was rough. I was selfish. I was not good with communication and impossible when it came to compromise. I had become pretty good at being a self-sufficient *me* and had no clue how to become part of a *we*.

Luckily, God paired me with a patient partner. Over time, I developed my skills and capabilities—communication, compromise, patience, kindness—and the results just kept getting better. I began to trust in my ability to be in a relationship and figure things out, no matter what came our way. This willingness to try and to possibly fail also helped me trust my partner more.

When I started The Restoration Project, I had no idea what it took to run a business. I had corporate experience and had been a self-motivated salesperson, so I knew some of my experience would translate, but more than anything, I had a deep desire and strong will to help and serve great leaders, teams, and organizations. I set out with dreams and ideas but no formal plan—and hit roadblock after roadblock.

Had I not held on to my desires and beliefs and had faith, I wouldn't have made it. It's been a challenging journey. Each failure or roadblock has served as an opportunity for me to learn more about myself and to acquire new skills. It has developed my competency around being a business owner, something you just can't know how to do until you actually do it. No amount of telling or learning can prepare you for what you will face.

We need to have the capability and results to trust ourselves, but when we set out to do something new, we have to remember that competence will be developed over time. Lean into the process and rely on coaches and mentors. Focus on who you are becoming and what you are learning and, pretty soon, the results will come. If you find yourself in a situation where you don't trust yourself, consider that it may be a new situation and that trust will be developed over time. Be patient in the process. That's hard to do in a world of quick wins and instant gratification. Learning, strength, growth, and sustainability come in the process of building our competence to get to the results, not in the results themselves. Have you heard the saying, "Life's a journey, not a destination"? Remember that.

Now is the time to push past your fear and your lack of self-trust. Let all of that fall away and let your heart and mind be open to dream again. Expand beyond all of your perceived limitations as you answer the questions in the following exercise. You have your whole life to come back to reality. Allow yourself the pleasure to dream in this moment and embrace this process with the childlike wonder you once had.

YOUR DREAMS

Take some time to explore (and enjoy) the following questions:

- What are the deep longings you've consistently ignored?
- If you could do anything, what would you do?
- If you could be anyone, who would you be?
- Who are you at your best? (What are you doing and how are you feeling when you're at your best?)
- How would you like people to describe you when you're not around or remember you when you're gone?

YOUR IDEAL VISION OF YOU

The answers to these questions form the foundation of an ideal vision of you and your life. Mark this page. Keep coming back to these questions as you evolve and grow—in each new year, in each new season of life. You can reflect on these questions to keep bringing yourself back to who you want to be and to realign yourself to your path of reaching your potential.

If you're up for it, consider taking a break from the book and spend a few days building a vision board using the answers to these questions.

Pick out photos and words that represent this ideal vision of you and your life, and put it somewhere you can see it. When we are specific and intentional about our vision, we naturally start to move toward it, even without specific goals (which will come later).

I love doing this reflection and vision board exercise with teenagers. There is so much of ourselves and our lives left unexplored at that age. It's fun to help teens become aware of their passions and gifts and consider who they are at their best. One of my clients expressed that she would like people to describe her as calm. She realized that to be perceived as calm, she actually has to *be* calm (in mind, body, and spirit), and to do that, she needs to spend more time in nature. She had never consciously made that connection until doing this exercise. Since then, she has filled her vision board with her favorite nature photos and spent more time outside.

In my most recent personal adventure with these questions, I revealed that I want people to describe me as peaceful and connected. The pace at which I have been living and working does not allow for that to be a reality. I have been rushing from task to task, which makes it difficult to connect with people. My energy in all that rushing is hurried and disjointed. When I shared this aspiration with my husband and friends, they graciously pointed out that the energy I bring into a space is rarely aligned with the word *peaceful*. As a fellow traveler on the journey, I have work to do right alongside you.

Creating this vision for ourselves allows us to see the gaps between where we are today and that ideal vision. In identifying the gaps, we can start to see the steps we need to take and the sacrifices we need to make to live out that ideal . . . or not. There are naturally gaps between our intentions and our actions, and there may always be, but the more we do this exercise, the fewer in number there will be; and the width of those gaps will be lessened. These questions will change our perception of ourselves and what we want out of life—which leads us into the final two questions we will explore in this chapter.

THE DEFINITION AND PROGRESSION OF SUCCESS

Your definition of success has likely been influenced by your parents, friends, culture, and the people you spend the most time with. It typically consists of things like what we want, what we think we should have, what we believe will make us happy, and what we think we should achieve or accomplish. Based on what you've learned so far in your exploration of this chapter, that definition has likely been challenged or maybe even changed entirely. So, let's explore it.

YOUR DEFINITION OF SUCCESS

What does success mean to you?
If you have difficulty putting things down on paper, consider the elements just listed that a definition of success usually includes. There is no right or wrong answer, and remember that your definition can and should change. As you change, it will change. In different seasons of your life, your definition may be different. Again, putting these elements on paper will allow you to be more intentional about the way you live, lead, and work from here.

When we are young, our definition of success may be in line with figuring out who we are, accomplishing our goals, and getting established. They include things like finding a career we enjoy, meeting someone we want to spend our life with, building a good life together, and buying our dream home.

As we move through life and these things become our reality, or our desires change to something different, our definition of success changes. Many people's definition of success may surround their career, travel, and other big dreams, until they have a family and want to pour their time and energy into their kids.

For others, there is a deeper shift. They meet their definition of success and still long for something deeper. They stay present to those longings and in pursuit of what those longings are calling them to. Success becomes less about how they are seen and what they accomplish. Less about outward success. There is a turn inward. A desire for alignment, peace, and deeper meaning—to contribute and add value in a more fulfilling way.

As we move out of our working years and face retirement, we see definitions of success shift into enjoyment and investment in the next generation. We are more comfortable with who and where we are. Our focus and definition of success continues to move increasingly toward a focus on others and the world around us and toward leaving a legacy.

If your definition of success feels very *you* focused, I challenge you to think deeper. A self-focused definition of success is typically driven by fear and insecurity. A healthy and whole definition of success considers how you will contribute and impact others and the world around you. Take a look at your definition and make adjustments accordingly.

REVEALING YOUR DEFINITION OF SUCCESS AND FACING YOUR MORTALITY

When walking clients through their definition of success, there are always realizations that come up. First, the definition they have been pursuing is not theirs and, in some ways, is the opposite of what they really want. Second, their real desires and the way they are living are not aligned. We say we want a bigger title and more responsibility at work, but we aren't willing to make the sacrifices required of our family. We say that a happy family and good relationships are important, but they only get our leftover time and energy. We say success equals peace, but we are unwilling to say no and clear our calendars.

These misalignments and difficult trade-offs lead us into a question that forces us to face our mortality. Sometimes, it takes extreme measures to get us to break our bad habits or shift old ways of thinking and comfortable patterns.

The Bhutanese people are known to be the happiest people on earth because they think about death regularly. Yes, it seems morbid, but I know this is true because I've experienced it myself! A few years back, a group of friends and I started the "One Word" practice to set intentions for the new year from the book *One Word That Will Change Your Life* by Jon Gordon. In this exercise, you don't just pick a word; you allow a word to reveal itself to you. There are questions you can use to guide you, but I used my meditation and prayer practices to allow the word to be revealed. Guess what came up? *Death.* Yes, you read that right.

I resisted that word. Hard. It just kept showing up. That's how I knew it was my word. I typically don't like the words that are revealed or pick me because they challenge me in an uncomfortable way. This word, though, would be extra difficult to explain to others and seemed like an extremely dark contrast from where I was a year ago, when my word was *play.*

If I'm honest, I feared what the word *death* would hold for me and force me to face. Finally, after sharing with a few people what it could mean, I decided to come out with it and accept it. Upon studying the word, I discovered the research that showed how facing our own death can help us live more fully. It was also revealed to me—through thinking, reading, and reflecting—the lengths we go to, especially in the United States, to shy away from thinking about, talking about, or honoring the process of death.

By disconnecting ourselves from the reality that life is short, we put things off, make excuses, and fall into patterns of numbing out (using TV, food, alcohol, shopping, gossip, and other reality escapes to keep us distracted from our own thoughts and feelings). It became clear to me that I, like many others, was using my perceived longevity to put off doing things I wanted to and should have been doing in the here and now. I was allowing myself to get distracted from what is truly most important.

So here we are. You only get one life. None of us is guaranteed a tomorrow. In one year alone, I had three close friends get a terminal diagnosis or die unexpectedly, all before the age of forty-five. Yes, it is uncomfortable and probably even terrifying to consider the fact that you may not be here tomorrow. I want you to sit with that truth because it will force you to consider the question in the next exercise more deeply. It will reveal to you where there are misalignments in what you really believe to be important and how you are living. So settle in and sit with this question for a while. Come back to it until you know in your heart you have come to the right place.

YOUR MORTALITY

It's not easy, but take a moment to really dig into the following question, welcoming the truths and insights it gives you.

- What will matter most in the end?

THE REALITIES OF FACING OUR MORTALITY

If you are anything like the hundreds of people that I've held space for in exploring this question, new insights and ways of thinking were likely revealed to you. Hard truths will lead to the sacrifices required to adjust your priorities in a way that will honor what will matter most in the end.

Many clients have pursued money while sacrificing their health and well-being. Many are pursuing status while sacrificing relationships. Others are pursuing favor at the sacrifice of their own peace. Tied to the previous question, some are trying to meet someone else's definition of success while sacrificing their values, who they are, and what is important to them.

Whether you believe it in this moment or not, this is the truth: Each of us is here for a specific purpose. You have a calling on your life, but you have to allow it to be revealed to you. If you have and continue to make time and space for exploring these questions and answering them honestly, you will continue to move closer to that purpose and calling. It won't look like anyone else's because only you have your unique gifts, perspectives, and experiences to contribute to this world.

Release your logical mind and allow yourself to reexamine or even reexplore the questions in this chapter with your heart. Allow yourself to dream. Allow yourself to reconnect with that innocent part of yourself, your inner child, the one who had ideas and feelings that were untainted by and untethered to this world.

Yes, you have a real life and real responsibilities. We will bring all of that back eventually, but in this time and in this place, allow yourself to set those aside. Open back up to the possibilities. To truly live a wholehearted and aligned life and existence, you must allow yourself to tap into something beyond logic. It may feel impossible or scary, and that's OK. Challenge yourself to expand your potential. Feel your passion for life come back. Allow yourself to dream again.

CREATING YOUR PERSONAL VISION

Go back and review all that you've put down on paper up to this point in this chapter. Your next step is to pull all of those things into a form that you can get your arms around and that makes sense to you.

You may be sick of me saying this by now, but there is no right way to do this. I use this process each year to build a new vision board. I answer all of these questions, then look at the statements and start to bring them together and to life on poster board. My boards consist of words, pictures, phrases, quotes, Bible verses, checkboxes with goals (like for the number of books I want to read), and other fun and creative ways to measure quantitative goals or the outcomes I seek.

Putting it all together in a way that you can see every day has a few benefits. First, it's a great way to start your day with intention. It serves as a reminder for you to come back to these things when life is feeling out of control. Second, by making it visible, your vision board gives you a chance to reflect on and celebrate progress.

Many of us have gone through life without clear intentions and goals to this point, so we have to develop a system and process for keeping them top of mind, changing them, and celebrating progress, so we can stick with them. You will be distracted, and you will get busy. You will see things other people have and want, so you need a visible reminder to recenter yourself on what's most important to you.

It's also important to make this process real and visible, because you need to share what you have learned and where you are going next with those you love, respect, and admire. Sharing allows you to refine your ideas and creates a network of support and accountability, so you can be lovingly reminded when you get off track. Feeling stuck and don't know where to go next? Just start! Or if you want to be part of a community, get a group together and workshop this chapter. You will learn as you go!

REFLECT ON YOUR JOURNEY

- What have you learned, unlearned, or relearned in this chapter?
- What has been most valuable to you?
- What one thing will you commit to doing differently going forward?
- Who can you invite in to keep you accountable?

CHAPTER 10

Asking for Input

Each of us has blind spots. No matter how evolved we are on our self-awareness journey and regardless of how many assessments, tests, and coaching and therapy sessions we've had, we always will have blind spots. That's why we need other people in our life to speak truth in kindness to us. The Bible says that iron sharpens iron. We form relationships to help each other evolve and become better.

In Chapter 5, we talked a lot about gathering feedback. If you are feeling uncomfortable about the idea of asking for input right now, go back to that chapter for some key reminders about why this is important and how to do it well. As we did with that step of gathering feedback, I want you to make a list of people you love, respect, and admire. This list may look a little different because we are seeking input on our vision, and you want people who will be thoughtful and honest about how they see you and will actively challenge your vision. Instead of including only family and friends, consider talking with mentors, leaders, coworkers, community members, and other people in your life you aspire to be more like.

First, we will reach out for insight into how others see us, then we will ask for feedback on our vision. These observations may change the way you go about pursuing your vision. People without our biases and assumptions might see actions, options, or a better path that we cannot see. Others may also have a more realistic idea of where and how wide our gaps are because they see things from a different perspective.

This input has been so helpful to me as I've continued to grow in my life and my career. As I share my vision and ask about my unique gifts, people point out things right in front of me that I have missed. These things sometimes seem small and simple, but they are hard to see when we are in them. Getting this input and feedback from others has made profound differences in the success of my business and in my personal growth and development.

A small, professional example that has had a profound impact on me is this: In the early days of my business, I used to field all the coaching inquiries myself. Pretty soon, I was spending a ton of time talking with people who did not turn into clients. I also had clients that I didn't enjoy working with. In discussing this with my coach, he pointed out that I could have someone else on the team handle the inquiring and intake process to ensure I didn't spend my time vetting those who were not serious (and I could spend more time with paying clients). Plus, having someone else vet for the right fit would ensure I had a book full of clients I enjoy. This small change has made a profound difference to me and the business.

A larger, more personal example is this: Within the last two years, I have shifted my own definition of success quite dramatically. I desire to be more present and experience things more fully, and to have more peace. But it took an outsider to point out that given my packed schedule, I wouldn't have that peace. After that realization, I limited my schedule to a certain number of clients per day and challenged myself to think about what other adjustments I needed to make to turn getting and keeping peace into a reality. Success was about quantity and money, and so I had built my habits and practices in life and work around that definition. Now that success had shifted to presence and peace, real changes needed to be made in how I thought and acted.

All of us need others to speak into our life and work. No matter how wise and evolved we become, we still can't see what we can't see when we're in the middle of our own situation. It's just the way it is. You don't have to share your vision with others if you don't want to. I know it can be scary. But if you choose not to, you will not get to the richness and depth required to reach your full potential. It's as simple as that. You get to choose: keep it in the dark and get where you get or bring it to the light and guarantee you will go further.

Aim to share your vision with at least three people. Find people who have different life experiences and perspectives and are at different places in their own life and work journey.

GAINING PERSPECTIVE ON BLIND SPOTS AND UNIQUE GIFTS

Let's explore your blind spots and unique gifts using the following two questions: "What do you see that I don't?" and "What are my unique gifts?" The first question is centered around the habits, patterns, and intentions that you may not be aware of. I have found that it is a powerful way to keep the possibilities for sharing open and expansive. If the recipient is having a hard time thinking of something, maybe suggest some examples from your life or think of a different question that will get them to the answers you are looking for.

For the second question, challenge the recipient to think deeply. Allow the first answers to come and then ask them to consider what you are better at than anyone else they know. The answer doesn't have to be about something you do; it can also be based on who you are. Maybe you make people feel safe. Maybe you have good energy. As they are answering, you will feel in yourself which ones are most important and ring most true. You will know when you are getting past the surface-level answers.

SEEING PAST BLIND SPOTS TO YOUR UNIQUE GIFTS

This can be an uncomfortable exercise, but it can be so helpful for our learning and growth. Open yourself up and invite people in. Allow people to share their perspective of you, and accept their words as a gift. Give them space to share, and after they share their initial answers, ask them if they can think of anything else. The second and deeper answer can be the most helpful.

Ask people the following questions as they relate to your vision:

- What do you see that I don't?
- What are my unique gifts?

GATHERING INPUT ON YOUR VISION

Now that you have gained some insight on your gifts, let's gather input on your vision. We'll do that by asking the following two questions: "Why is this vision possible?" and "What could get in the way?" Before we do that, though, spend some time painting the picture of your vision for the persons with whom you are sharing it, and limit any questions, explanations, and discussion at this point. You want to stay in the ideation phase of the process—the *what* of your vision—and not get into the specifics of *how* yet. As with the last set of questions, dig deeper than the initial answers. Allow yourself to spend some time here, and give the other person time to think and consider. You can ask both of these questions in one sitting, but start with why the vision is possible before moving into what might get in the way.

When asking for input on your vision, it's imperative to start with the positive by first asking what's possible and what things could go right. As humans, we naturally tend to go negative. So we need to keep our focus on all the possibilities that lie within our vision and all the reasons that it could work. This is also why we ask for input, because other people can see the things we cannot, the paths that are not obvious to us. They can open us up to new opportunities. Let yourself explore and dream around the possibilities.

Once you have firmly rooted yourself in a vision of what's possible, then it's time to bring the realities and obstacles back in. This will expand your thinking and challenge you to see things in new ways. As we get older, we become more risk averse and tend to be more cynical about people and the world—about possibilities in general. We can become dream killers. We naturally fear change. We allow minor hurdles or challenges to become reasons why we can't do something. We allow comfort to take over, or use comparison to say that if others can't do something then we can't either. Feedback can clear all that up. Insight from others can force us to confront the difference between real obstacles and what might simply be an excuse or a fear. Feedback can also reignite our passion and give us the confidence boost we need to move ahead.

For example, as I'm writing this book, I feel called to work with more leaders who have the authority and influence to make systemic change, people I would normally feel intimidated by. The feelings and thoughts alone are enough to get in the way of my making this a reality, and I picture people asking me, "Who do you think you are?" or "How could they possibly benefit from working with you?" As I worked with my coach to make the list of people who came to mind, I set that little voice aside. New names and faces came to mind when I expanded my view instead of restricting it. This also helped me see obstacles in a new way.

Most of my obstacles were rooted in fear and limiting beliefs, and as I shared my vision and desires with others, they helped me see that excuses were holding me back, not reality. They reinforced the positive change they had witnessed in my work, shared the unique gifts they saw in me and the way they believed I could support systemic change, and then started sharing with me why this was possible and what I could do as a next step. It was just me getting in my own way of my dreams. The real obstacles were more like this: I don't know how to get a hold of these people and can't find their contact information. Well, then I can build another plan using my network and other people I know to find a way. I can put my intentions and dreams out into the universe and see what connections might be made. I realized in using this exercise myself that there were no real obstacles for me in this situation. Only myself.

You may be facing some concrete challenges. You may not have the finances for your dream. The timing may not be right. Your other obligations may prevent you from turning your vision into a reality. You may be physically unable to make your vision a reality. These limitations are real. You have to determine which can be put into a plan and which really can't be overcome.

Remember when I told you that I wanted to work in the nonprofit sector or serve people in a meaningful way, and my professor gently reminded me of all the student debt I had racked up? I kept my vision *and* accepted my current circumstances. Keeping the vision helped me make strategic decisions about what I did next, skills I acquired, actions

I took, books I read, ways I approached the job I had, and many other things that prepared me for serving in the way that I get to today.

Why is all this important? Because most of the clients I encounter have never let themselves dream. They gave up on their vision, hopes, and desires years ago, as so many people have. And we wonder why we feel so unfulfilled and unsettled! Others have been hurt by their dreams; they want something so much and the circumstances of life continue to get in the way of making that vision or dream a reality. I understand why we stop dreaming, but this severely limits our potential and the mark we can make in the world. This process of exploring, in and of itself, refines our spirit and deepens our wisdom in meaningful ways.

YOUR VISION

Create space and dream away with a friend or two or three by sharing your vision and then gathering input:

- Why is this vision possible?
- What could get in the way?

EVALUATING THE INPUT WE RECEIVE AND MAKING ADJUSTMENTS

Look at your answers from the preceding two exercises. How are you feeling? What are you thinking? How might you want or need to adjust your original vision based on the feedback you received? Remember that input is simply a contribution of information. You don't have to agree with it, and you don't have to do anything with it. This entire process is about helping you strengthen and refine your vision, helping you see your blind spots, and giving you additional perspective. It's up to you to pull all of that input together, take a look at it, and decide what's worth keeping, adjusting, and taking action on. Let the rest go.

Here's the reality: We are all different, and we are called to different things. What works for me may not work for you. We are not seeking validation or even opinions from others. We are seeking information. By inviting people in, they will openly share their recommendations and point of view with you. You must break free of your need to be understood and instead decide for yourself what is true for you.

In those first few months of business, I allowed others to influence the language the business used, the nature of our engagements, and the structure of our offerings in a way that went against what I inherently felt was aligned to me and my integrity. I was seeking validation from other leaders I respected, and I wanted our business to have opportunities. Instead of using language and structure that felt natural to us, we took the advice of many business leaders and conformed to traditional business language, as well as coaching and consulting structures. For many months I went against what I knew was right for me, for us. As a result, we were attracting the wrong clients, reducing the impact of our work, and taking the life out of the process for our team. Energetically, it was all wrong.

The people sharing these ideas were not ill-intentioned, and their ideas were not bad; but their ideas just weren't right for me or our team. It was a good idea for me to reach out for feedback, but I could have done a better job of considering the source of the feedback I was looking for and, most importantly, a better job at discerning what feedback I allowed in and used based on what felt right to me. So that's what I'm asking you to do now—return to all the input you've gathered and wade through it with the question, "Does this feel right for me?"

Herein lies the challenge: We need other people's input to refine our ideas *and* we must stay in our own integrity and decide what's best for us. So many of us have been conditioned to do what other people say, so we can please or appease them, or we conform to the majority in order to belong and avoid judgment. But we compromise our values and work against ourselves in the process.

Growing up, we are told no by authority figures as they strove to help us find our bearings and boundaries and to keep us safe. As we get older, we forget that we are safe, and we continue to listen to the voices telling us how to think, speak, act, and be, even when it goes against what we know to be right or good for us, even when our inner voice is screaming something else at us.

This becomes especially dangerous as people acquire authority, power, and influence. If you haven't healed your people-pleasing and worthiness wounds, you will be taken advantage of. You will be put in positions time and time again that compromise your own integrity. Eventually, you will resign yourself to a victim mentality, or you will become bitter, resentful, and hard-hearted. We can't let this happen. We must remain open to input and discern for ourselves what is necessary and true for us.

BEING OPEN WHILE STAYING TRUE TO OUR VISION AND UNIQUE CALL

Being in the world but not of the world is a challenge. Being with people and not allowing them to influence us away from our call is difficult. Being open to the input of others and seeing it simply as information while still making our own choice shows a level of courage, maturity, and discipline that few leaders ascend to.

Opening yourself up in this way will help you sharpen your relationship-building skills and deepen the relationships themselves. We are too often scared to show people who we really are. By hiding and putting on a facade, we prevent ourselves from reaching our potential and experiencing the deep, meaningful, and loving relationships that could be available to us. To trust others, we must trust ourselves first. I hope that through this process, you are building that self-trust muscle.

Be mindful and realistic about who you can trust and with what. We only extend our trust to another to the level and extent someone else is capable of receiving our trust. Some people are not ready or willing to hold our deeper realities. Do not share with people who are not able to keep private things to themselves. There is no black-and-white answer around who you can trust, with what, and how deep you should go. That is up to you to discern and learn.

Balancing that truth, keep in mind that one of the best ways to build trust and relationships is by being open and vulnerable, by sharing first. Everyone is comfortable at a different level. In the workplace I often talk with teams about the spectrum of professional → personal → private. In the course of a normal workday, people don't often share the private parts of their lives. Within those sections of the spectrum, there are also varying degrees of comfortability in sharing.

For example, when someone is going through a divorce, they may not be willing to share what specifically is happening or even that they are going through a divorce. They may only be willing to share that they are going through a personal matter that has them under stress. They may not desire for others to know, they may not think the people around them want to be bothered with their personal life, they may not trust others not to share or gossip about them, or all of the above. A situation like this is a deeply personal and individual choice that all of us need to make for ourselves.

We hold all of that as a personal choice, knowing that people will perceive us in a certain way based on what we share and what we do not. If someone is hesitant to share anything about their personal life, people may perceive them as guarded and cold and may have a difficult time connecting with and approaching them. On the other hand, if someone is sharing openly about their private life, people may not trust that they would keep the personal matters of others confidential. You have to share in a way that is best for you. Find a place that will create the least amount of worry on your end and still allow for some connection through disclosure.

SHARING WITH INTENTION AND RESPECT

I tend to err on the side of oversharing, while my husband likes to keep personal matters to himself. Within our marriage, we have had to do a lot of work to find a dynamic that works for us, and we have to be intentional about our sharing. When we are more open, we tend to share things we're thinking about but not necessarily going to take action on that could startle the other person. We expose the inner thoughts and parts of ourselves that others may think about but never say out loud and that can scare people.

People who are more open also tend to process more with their partner and others around them, putting the emotional and mental weight of what they are thinking and feeling on others, which can cause strain on the relationship. I have to think about what I want to tell my husband and how. I use my coach and therapist to do most of the "dumping and processing," so that with my husband I can simply share what I'm thinking about and how I'm feeling (or not, if I don't need to) to help us maintain a healthier relationship dynamic. This way, the hours we spend together can be for dreaming and playing rather than commiserating and processing. It works for us.

My husband is more introverted and would rather not talk about most things. As an empath, I can pick up on the fact that he's stressed or upset. Early in our relationship when he didn't tell me why, I assumed it was something I did wrong. Now he knows that he can simply tell me, "I'm pretty stressed about work but I have a session set up with my coach and I'm going to try not to let it bother me." This clears the air that it isn't me, shows me that he's actively working through things, and invites me to give a little grace if he's not himself in our interactions.

When we share with others, it's important to remember to share while maintaining ownership. We are creating awareness of what we are thinking or feeling, but we are not necessarily asking someone else to fix it or expecting to dump that energy and those feelings on another person. You know what that feels like, right? When you meet up with a friend and they talk most of the time telling you about all their problems? They leave feeling lighter and energized, and you feel heavy and drained. We don't want that!

When we are in the mode to blame or complain, we are putting our energy on other people. We are abdicating our ownership and responsibility in a situation. There are times when we just need to vent, and that is OK, but it's important to be mindful that we aren't doing that often. There are also times when we just want someone else to feel sorry for us or to validate us or fix our problems. If we are seeking energy from another person in this way, it is important to remember that the interaction is likely draining that person.

Being in relationships with others is complex and complicated. We learn by doing it, and we won't always get it right. The good thing is that even when we mess up, we can keep trying. In working through things together, we form strong bonds. We learn about others and ourselves, so each interaction can get better and better. Inviting others into our lives and stories, and connecting deeply, can create positive change and even transformation.

At this point, you have learned from others about their perception of you and leaned into it. You have learned about yourself by being open to their point of view and being in a relationship or relationships with others. You have been given new ideas and insights from others about your vision. Now that you have all of this information in front of you, it's up to you to decide what you do with it. What feels good? What feels true and aligned to you? Once you have answered these questions and incorporated this feedback into what you have learned, then you will be ready to move to the next step.

REFLECT ON YOUR JOURNEY

- What have you learned, unlearned, or relearned in this chapter?
- What has been most valuable to you?
- What one thing will you commit to doing differently going forward?
- Who can you invite in to keep you accountable?

CHAPTER 11

Learning New Ways

The last chapter of this section is where we start to make a turn toward action. As a reminder, Part 2 of this book has been all about restoring intention—digging deep into what is meaningful and valuable to us, envisioning what's possible from deep within, and going deep into our connections to explore what others think and see for us. If you have given time, energy, and devotion to these steps, you will see yourself with new eyes and will have discovered new things.

With these discoveries, you now have to make a choice. Do you commit to learning and to new ways of thinking, believing, behaving, and being, or do you remain tied to who you were before? This is a point of transformation that takes intentional choice and a great deal of energy. Allowing yourself to be transformed, to become different, to surrender, and to accept a new reality is going to take real commitment.

The questions and reflections in this chapter will bring up the trade-offs and changes required to become more aware of and conscious of your choices. By coming face-to-face with what will be different and leaning into learning new ways, you will be able to root yourself in new patterns that will carry you through those moments where you may want to resist or turn back. This is a key part of healing and forward progress.

Through our life journey, we may become aware of what could be different, but it isn't until we force ourselves to face the reality of how we will need to change and what the trade-offs will be that we can really embrace and carry out what we see. In the previous steps, we worked on closing the gap between awareness and understanding. Now, we face another chasm, this one between understanding and commitment, that requires our choice, our energy, and our action.

Considering all you have learned in the last few chapters, what new possibilities do you see for yourself and your life? What new things do you want? How do you want to be different? Make sure those things are in front of you. I would encourage you to put your vision board in front of you or write these things down as you consider the questions in this chapter.

Sometimes, we are resistant to writing things down because that makes them real. In this case, writing them down gives them power and allows us to give these things space as we consider the questions that will allow us to commit to them. You can always change your mind. You can always cross them off. Just put them on paper.

THE IMPORTANCE OF KNOWING WHY WE WANT NEW THINGS

There are two reasons we should know why we want new things for our life before we go about pursuing them. First, we want to be clear about why we want these new things, so we are sure the reason comes from us and our heart and not from the influence of someone else. Second, when we tie our desire for something to the reason we want it, we are more likely to stick with it when things get tough. In short, we will be more committed. Knowing why will help prepare you to more successfully see it through. Also, walk yourself through the impact these new things will have on you and the world around you.

Thinking, reflecting, anticipating, and envisioning are important parts of the process as we move toward action. These steps prepare our hearts and our minds. They build our strength, courage, and resolve. When we don't make time to think through why we want to make change or what impact it could have, it's easy to give up as things get hard. And they will, because change is always difficult. Making time to prepare our hearts and minds for change allows us to be better equipped to stay committed when that's what we need and have clarity about when we need to let go or pivot.

EXPLORING YOUR WANTS

Why do you want these new things?
Write whatever comes up first. Don't allow yourself to overthink the answer. When your heart speaks to you, it often doesn't make sense. If you just can't seem to get out of your head, and you find yourself stuck, close your eyes and use the opposite hand you normally write with to write out the answer. This is a great technique I use. It engages a different part of your brain and allows you to move past your ego or tendency to overthink and makes for a more authentic answer.

There may be some logical reasoning infused in your answers, which is great. We are also looking for the emotional appeal of this question. Can you feel why these new things are important to you? Sit with those feelings. Allow them to soak in. These feelings are something you can come back to when fear or limiting beliefs creep back in and tempt you to go back to old things and old ways.

continued

What impact could these new things have (on you, on your relationships, in your life, on your career, etc.)?

Write out what will be different. How will the impact of these new things change you, your experience, your environment, your life? What new outcomes will be possible? What will be great? What will be challenging? Allow yourself some space to explore impacts. Give yourself time to envision how things will look and feel different.

Again, being intentionally and consciously aware of your answers and working to anticipate and understand some of what you will experience will help you stay grounded as things start to shift and that, in turn, will help you remain committed to positive change even when the journey gets challenging.

LISTENING TO YOUR HEART BEFORE MAKING DECISIONS

Building my business has been one of the most challenging things I've done. My partner and I experienced fast growth at the beginning, and I hadn't thought through the two key questions on exploring my wants as we discussed changes and new ways of doing things. In a short time, things didn't feel good, and I found myself feeling burned out and frustrated.

When I started The Restoration Project, I had a vision for how I could support leaders and organizations to live, lead, and work with meaning. I wasn't sure exactly how it would look or who my clients would be, but I knew this was my calling and had faith that God would bring me the people He wanted me to serve. I had a vision and plans for services, offerings, and growth, and I was also working hard to maintain a new work-life balance that I'd never had in the corporate world. I wanted to build a successful business *and* live a meaningful and fulfilling life. In the past, I had been solely focused on work, which had left me burned out, frustrated, and unhappy.

I had figured out that working with clients and serving others was where I got most of my energy, so I started reaching out to executives and organizations I admired that had similar values and asked what issues they were facing. This was how I received some of my first clients for individual coaching, workshops, and consulting engagements. Like most new businesses, we learned as we had new opportunities, and we started to build some frameworks and processes as we grew.

As more clients and opportunities came to us, we just kept saying yes. We brought new people onto the team to support internal efforts and client work. At one point, some of the team members expressed their concern that there wasn't a clear plan, and they didn't understand their role. We invested time, money, and energy building out more structure, systems, and processes. During that period, it started to become clear that the hopes and desires I had for the organization and how it would work were not aligned with some of the expectations of our team members.

We were moving down a path to change my role, mostly removed from client work, to focus on strategy, business development, and coaching team members. I was so fixated on making it work with the team members we had brought on that I didn't see another way, even though I was deeply unhappy about the work this would mean I would have to do each day. My business coach could see that in me. At the eleventh hour of changing the structure and duties, he asked me to think back to why I founded The Restoration Project and consider the same two questions we just reviewed in this chapter: Why did I want these new things? What impact would it have on me?

At that moment, I felt a weight lifted, and I broke down. I didn't want any of these new things, especially considering the reality that I wouldn't be able to do much client-facing work going forward. So he courageously asked me why I was pursuing this model. I told him I felt like it was my only option. He patiently and graciously pointed out that I was headed back down the road to unhappiness if I didn't consider what I wanted to be doing and if I let what everyone else wanted get in the way. He even challenged me to consider that I would be going against God's calling on my life by putting what others wanted in front of what I felt called by Him to do.

At first, this all felt pretty selfish on my part, but with encouragement from my coach, I moved forward, compelled by the vision God had given me for this business. My business partner and I had some tough decisions and discussions ahead of us. In the end, we decided that it was most important for everyone that we do the work in the way we felt called to do it. If that meant that it went back to just the original three of us on the team (me, my business partner, and our teammate Sarah), then that's the way it would have to be. While our team did shrink in size because of these changes, I'm happy to report that internally and externally, it feels better than ever because we were true to ourselves and are now in alignment.

In each of our lives, we will have these critical moments, these opportunities to follow our calling or follow someone else's desires for our life. If we aren't proactively seeking and planning for what we want, someone will make plans for what they want us to do. That's all fine and good as long as it aligns with our unique gifts, desires, and the call of our own heart.

EXPLORING WHAT YOU FEEL CALLED TO DO

What do you want to be when you grow up? We start being asked this very big question at a very young age. As someone who has mostly explored and wandered their way through life, I have been intimidated and annoyed by this question. I felt so much pressure to have a step-by-step plan and everything figured out, when in reality, I just wanted to try a bunch of things and see what worked.

At some point in my life, I succumbed to the pressure and stopped exploring and creating things. I stopped listening to my call and started listening to everyone else. In my life and career, I asked others for advice and readily took it with no regard as to whether it felt right to me or not. I climbed a ladder and walked a path, then looked around one day wondering, "How did I get here?"

I think this happens for all of us at some point in our lives. Many of us don't come to this realization that we have followed the call of others instead of our own, until much later in life or even on our deathbed. I don't want that to be you. Let's rediscover and explore your call now.

YOUR CALLING

Take some time to think about the following question:

What do you want to create in the world?

This is a *big* question. It's one that can and will likely change. Don't overwhelm yourself with it. Have fun with it! At this very moment, what are you passionate about? What do you want to use your time, energy, and talents for?

I encourage you to revisit this question every day to establish your focus at a micro-level on how you impact the world around you. It's also one you can build a larger and more long-term vision around, based on where you're at in life, what your priorities are, and what you're passionate about. For example, my answers are different when I add *today, this week, this month, this quarter, this year,* or *this lifetime* to the end of the question. Try it out and see what you come up with.

Having clarity on this question, what do you want to create in the world, will help you continue to evolve and be more intentional about the way you live, lead, and work. It will help you find meaning in even the most mundane of tasks. For instance, one of the most enduring answers to this question for me is "I want to create love and hope everywhere I go and with everyone I meet." That has been a guiding force in how I choose to show up each day and what I need to do to keep myself in a loving and hopeful place. It requires me to take care of my mental, emotional, physical, and spiritual health and drives routines, habits, and practices that help me do that, which has also released me from old patterns that were holding me back from showing up as I desired.

This answer also drives my attitude and approach (well, most days because hey . . . none of us is perfect and we all have tough days). Where I used to meet many things with "no" and resistance, now I work to keep an open mind and heart, see potential, and find a way to make positive change occur even in seemingly hopeless situations.

THE IMPORTANCE OF OTHERS IN LEARNING NEW WAYS

As we get clearer on what we want to create in the world, it's important that we move back out into a space of inviting others into our vision and desires. Tell others what you want to create in the world and why it's important to you. Especially when it feels like a long shot, you have to be willing to believe in your dream enough to share it with others and invite them in to help you make it real. What you want to create in the world may be different from the vision you shared earlier, but it may be similar. When I consider what I want to create in the world, I align more with my calling and who I want to *be*, and my vision is more aligned with what I want to *do*.

Take time to consider others who have a similar vision and what they have done. Read about them, study them, understand how they think and behave. Their lives can read as a blueprint for your own plan to live this out. If you can find someone in your circle who is creating something similar to what you want to create in the world, even better. Spend time with them! Maybe even ask them to mentor you.

When I think of loving and hopeful people whom I want to be more like and the impacts they've made on the world that are similar to those I'd like to create, I always come back to the following: Jesus, Mother Teresa, St. Thérèse of Lisieux, Martin Luther King Jr., the Dalai Lama, Henri Nouwen, Thomas Merton, and Father Richard Rohr. I have read their books, listened to their speeches, studied their lives and work, and picked up on how they spent their time and energy to remain loving and hopeful in even the darkest of times and situations. It has been imperative in my own life to remember that I am not walking this path alone. I am not the first and will not be the last. Studying saints and heroes of this caliber also keeps me hungry to work harder in those situations when I want to give up. I have faced nothing like these amazing humans have faced, and so if they could press on, I can find the strength to do it too.

I am also lucky to have a few mentors and coaches I get to interact with more regularly in real life who are a model for creating love and hope everywhere they go. I use these relationships as opportunities to dive deeper into learning about their lives and work and how they made the transition into who they are today. What are they reading? What are they practicing? What are they doing? I use my time with them to get very specific and honest about my own thoughts, feelings, habits, and patterns. We explore and evaluate them so that I can continue to evolve. Again, this has been an incredibly important part of my life and work journey. To have someone in your life who has walked a similar path and who can give you concepts, frameworks, context, and perspective that you just cannot see when you are walking your own path is so helpful and grounding.

We learn new ways of thinking, seeing, and doing not only by exploring new possibilities within ourselves but also by studying other people and perspectives. In doing so, we expand our potential, and that's why this step is so important. We want to give ourselves space to see all of our options and expand our horizons before we commit to action.

This chapter concludes Part 2 of this book. In Part 1, we walked through rebuilding our connection to ourselves and our identity. The work we did was centered around who we are, beyond the labels, and why we are the way we are. We explored the experiences and perceptions, beliefs and behaviors, patterns and influences that shaped us. In that process, we uncovered pieces that feel authentic and true, became aware of some things that were put on us by outside influences, and identified limiting beliefs and fears that are not true or no longer serve us and let them go.

Because we gained greater clarity in our identity, we moved into Part 2, which had us digging into and exploring our intentions. Our work in this part of the book was around what we see as possibilities, what we want, and what's meaningful to us. We made space for ourselves to explore our own hearts and minds, and we invited people we trust and respect to share their ideas and perspectives about what's possible for us.

My hope is that you have been able to identify so far what new things you want and your motivation behind wanting them, and home in on what you want to create in the world. Keeping all of those answers in mind, you now need to look in the mirror and evaluate what shifts you must make in your thinking, habits, and behaviors. We are ready to dive into Part 3, the final part of the book, and move from reflection and exploration into action.

REFLECT ON YOUR JOURNEY

- What have you learned, unlearned, or relearned in this chapter?

- What has been most valuable to you?

- What one thing will you commit to doing differently going forward?

- Who can you invite in to keep you accountable?

Aligning Action

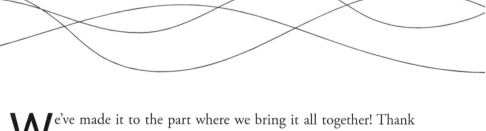

We've made it to the part where we bring it all together! Thank you for your patience and perseverance to this point. I know that this is deep, challenging work. It takes discipline and patience to sit with these questions and allow space for exploration and emergence to occur. In our society, we are driven by instant gratification, and we easily jump from incident to response. By giving yourself more time and space to reflect and dive deeper, I hope you see the importance and power of creating more space between incident and response, and the improved quality of thought and outcomes.

Now, it is time for action. Action requires courage and commitment. You have undoubtedly discovered things that have transformed you internally and which compel you to change external circumstances or yourself in some way. Facing those realities takes courage, and acting on them takes real commitment. In this part, we will determine what needs to change, develop an action plan, invite in support, walk through how to integrate and assess our progress, and finally end with a framework that will encourage and inspire you to share what you've learned.

When we are transformed internally, it's possible that even if our external circumstances remain the same, we are able to positively shift our perspective and impact everyone and everything around us in a new way. This is the work of being the change you want to see in the world, the saying often attributed to Mahatma Gandhi. When each of us shifts our focus from trying to change what we cannot control or to blame others for our circumstances and to having the courage and commitment to focus on our own personal growth, development, and transformation, we can literally change our world.

There are a few things I want to remind you of before we get started. First, you have to remember that action matters. You can have all the best of intentions to this point, but if you do not change your thoughts, beliefs, behaviors, and patterns, then none of it matters. Intention and action are two very different things, and when it comes to our lives and relationships, action is what will prove our commitment to ourselves, our relationships, and the world.

Second, as you embark on this journey of new patterns and habits, you will fall off the proverbial wagon. It's not a matter of if, but when. This is all part of the process. Don't get discouraged, and give yourself grace. Some of the patterns I am working to shift in myself have been with me for more than thirty years, and I know it's going to take time and consistent effort to shift them. Each time we fall is a chance to learn more about ourselves. Because of our propensity to fall off that wagon, we must be disciplined and committed, and we have to invite others into the journey with us for support and encouragement, but also to challenge us to keep going or pivot.

Third, don't hesitate to make these changes. We don't like change, so taking action on all that you have learned is going to be the part that you resist the most. There are real consequences when we start taking action. There is also a detrimental downside when we don't. Remember that our days are numbered. Having lost several good friends at a young age, I know deeply and intimately that we never know when it will be our time. Don't sit with these good intentions too long or until it's too late.

Lastly, getting through this part does not mean you are done. This is just the beginning of your journey to reach your potential, and it's a lifelong one. You will make commitments. Change and transformation will happen. New patterns will be integrated and become part of who you are. A new level of awareness will take place, and then you get to start the process all over again. Each new transition and change will help you to become your highest and truest self—that person you were created to be. With it comes the freedom, peace, passion, and hope that you are seeking. As you change for the good, everything else changes for the good around you.

Remember that while much of this work is for and about you, it's also about bringing you back to being in service to others and the world. When we consistently think, live, work, and act from a healthy and whole place, we bring health and wholeness to our relationships and the world around us. When we are healthy and whole, we can be of greater service to the world. That's what we were all created for and what we are wired to do. Our awareness and our sense of security free us to focus on and help others. So let's get to our work so we can get there!

CHAPTER 12

Determining What Needs to Change

Before we can jump into creating change, we must make time to explore what needs to change. We may get so excited to take action that we take action on the wrong thing or in the wrong direction, and then we don't see the progress we'd like and give up. Or we may discover that the step we need to take to change seems too hard, so we opt for something other than what we should do next. Using what we've learned in the previous chapters, we'll home in on what needs to change and the first and most impactful steps to take next. To illustrate this process, I am using a client that I call Susan as our guide.

When Susan went through this journey with me as a client, we discovered very clearly what needed to change, but when it came to taking action, she became very resistant. This may happen to you too. With change comes loss and sacrifice. Discomfort is inevitable. Even when we aren't happy with our current situation, we at least understand it.

A natural caretaker, Susan was a great mom and wife, an always-available friend, and someone you could always count on to volunteer for your event. She also had an incredibly important job and a highly influential role. Susan was very successful, but she had completely lost herself. Her focus had been on everyone else for so long that she resisted turning inward, talking about her needs, and had a hard time identifying what she wanted.

For most of our first sessions together, we focused on her work. She had transitioned into a new role, and she wanted to develop her influence and executive skills and ensure she was working on the right things and maximizing her impact. We took an inventory of her beliefs and behaviors. We discussed vision and priorities. Once we had those things all laid out (using many of the questions in the previous chapters), I asked her, "What needs to change in order for you to live more fully aligned to this vision we have created?"

She listed some behaviors, habits, and routines that needed to shift, which was great. We captured those, and I asked her to go back to her beliefs, because without making shifts in her heart and mind, the likelihood of fruitful action on the behavior part would probably not stick. To get work off her plate, for instance, she needed to believe in her heart and mind that delegating was a good thing for her and for those she was delegating to. Knowing we need to make these shifts sounds good in practicality, but when we get down to it, if we don't believe in them in our hearts and minds, we won't follow through. We will find excuses or not even realize we are holding on to things we could give away because we are blocked.

As a natural caretaker, Susan did not like to delegate anything to anyone because she didn't want to burden others. There may also have been a bit of a control issue—not believing that others could do it as well as she would and therefore not wanting to give it away. And of course, the "It's easier just to do it myself" theme came up too.

Susan and I processed these beliefs together. I shared alternative perspectives and asked her to recall the times she was grateful for something being delegated to her, so she could learn and grow. Through our conversation, I could sense things start to shift. We talked through how she could delegate things in a way that felt good to her and the other person involved. We walked through the nitty-gritty details of how this would go. This is often what we need to force ourselves to do to fully shift a belief and be committed to change.

The same things happened related to her desire to be more influential. There was a practical side of influence we explored, related to how she wanted to influence and whom. We made plans for that. But for her to be successful in influencing others, she had to believe in her heart and mind that she was influential. See how it's all tied together? We addressed the limiting beliefs she had about herself. We talked about the people she looked up to in this area. We envisioned what being influential in an authentic way might look and feel like. Again, I could sense the shifts start to take place as we worked through the limiting beliefs and talked about the specific details of how this would come to fruition.

Susan made great strides and sustainable shifts that positively impacted her, her team, and the overall organization. She made great progress, yet I knew we had another mountain to climb together. Before we get to that part, take some time to explore what you know needs to change based on the work you have done so far.

SHIFTS TO MAKE

As leaders and as humans, we have to be aware of what we are telling ourselves in our minds and believing in our hearts before we can create positive change that sticks.

- What needs to change in order for you to live more fully aligned?

Once you have your initial list down, go deeper.

- What heart shifts need to take place? (What old beliefs and ways of feeling need to change? What new patterns need to be instilled?)
- What mindset shifts need to happen? (What old ways of thinking need to go away? What new patterns of thinking need to be instilled?)

When we get to this part and are preparing to take action, we often equate action and change with the external and physical, when in reality, what is most often holding us back is what's happening inside us that we can't see. Before we can *do* something different, sometimes we have to *be* something different so that *doing* sticks.

When I decided to write a book, there was a lot in my heart and mind that needed to shift before I could break my behavioral patterns and take different actions. For instance, one practice I implemented was scheduling writing time for an hour each morning. Sure, I put it on my calendar, but within one week, I wasn't sticking to it. I thought maybe it was my method, and instead of a little at a time, I was a person who needed to block off a whole chunk of time or a full day for writing. Wrong. I didn't stick to that either, and I wrote actually less per hour when I had the whole day set aside than when I was just writing for an hour each day.

I found that my issue had nothing to do with the behaviors, habits, routines, or practices and everything to do with my heart and mind. There was a lot there. When I challenged myself to really think about what my mind was telling me when I sat down to write, it was things like, "This is too hard," "You could be seeing clients and making money right now," "No one is going to read this book anyway." These and a million other negative stories were running through my mind, sometimes even under the radar of my awareness. So I continued to schedule things over my writing time or find other excuses not to write.

Yet when I checked in with my heart, I found fear. A lot of it. "What if people hate it?" "What if this is all for naught and the book doesn't even get published?" "Am I crazy to put my heart and soul onto paper and into the world like this—it seems unsafe?" Once again, these and a million other fears were swirling around in my head and my heart. I noticed that whenever I sat down to write, these fears made me anxious and uncomfortable. I would get all spun up, experience a complete block, and get very frustrated.

I had to take hold of and shift my heart and mind to move forward. So I had a long "talk" with myself about these things. Writing isn't hard for me. Maybe it is for others but not for me. For me, it's one of the easiest and most enjoyable things I get to do. Remembering this truth was powerful in creating a shift. I reminded myself of this each time I sat down and felt the anxiety melt away. I now looked forward to sitting down to write versus dreading it.

The hardest mindset shift I had to make was the one related to "You could be seeing clients and making money right now," because that was true. This book was an investment. There was only so much time in the day, so I did have to trade either client hours or my personal time to make it happen. This talk with myself took a lot longer to shift. I allowed myself to argue points back and forth about why the book was important, how important it was right now, and what the trade-offs could look like. Just as we work to compromise with others when making change, we have to give ourselves time and space to allow those arguments to play out until we can find common ground.

The heart shifts required in this area were much harder. I found myself deep in fear. So much so that at one point, the writing got completely stalled out. My editor kept checking in and gently nudging with no pressure. She was an angel through the process, knowing I needed positive encouragement. I had also shared with some friends and coaches that I was writing this book in case this exact thing happened. No amount of encouragement helped my heart shift. I was still stuck in fear.

Finally, one of my coaches forced me into action. She said the only thing that was going to get me out of this paralysis was to allow others into the manuscript. Not all of it but just a piece. I had been keeping it in the dark for so long, hugging it close in the dark corner, not allowing anyone to see it, and I had gotten comfortable there. She demanded I share it with her. I said, "OK, I'll send it as soon as we get off this call." She said, "No, you're going to send it to me right now."

She patiently waited for me to create a PDF and email her the first nine pages. Once she received it, she said she would be back in touch within the day when she'd had a chance to read it. She affirmed that I was on the right path and that writing was my gift, and she made me commit to sharing it with a handful of others. I could feel the fear bubble up to its highest point when I sent that PDF to her. While waiting for her response, I did everything to distract myself. When I received her note back, I felt the weight lift. This is the power of bringing our fears into the light and sharing them with others.

In subsequent shares, the fear dissipated even more. One of my friends let me know that she was going to read it, but she wasn't going to tell me whether or not she liked it because it wasn't her opinion that mattered.

Initially, I was caught off guard and offended. I felt the defensiveness and hurt rise up inside me. As we talked through it, I realized that she had given me a profound gift that helped me shed my last layers of fear to get this book across the finish line. She reminded me that this book is between me and God and that nothing else matters. I never set out to write it for anyone else, and it has been one of the most refining experiences of my life. I had lost sight of that in all of my fear, and I will be forever grateful for that moment and powerful reminder that I continue to carry into other areas of my life.

Once you have determined the heart and mindset shifts that need to be made in your life and work, and you are committed to them, we'll look at the behaviors, habits, routines, and practices that need to shift to help you embrace and live out this new, enhanced vision for yourself.

CHANGING YOUR BEHAVIORS, HABITS, ROUTINES, AND PRACTICES

Remember the start, stop, and continue method from Chapter 3? We're going to use it again here to look your behaviors, habits, routines, and practices that need to shift. List one to three items for start, stop, and continue in each of the following questions. For instance, list one to three behaviors you need to start, one to three you need to stop, and one to three you need to continue. I purposefully included "continue" in these examples because in the midst of change, you also need to keep in mind what can't or shouldn't change.

- What behaviors need to start, stop, and continue?
- What habits and routines need to start, stop, and continue?
- What practices need to start, stop, and continue?

My hope is that you have a long list, *and* you are free of fear and shame when you look at it. Each of us is a continuous work in progress, and this journey of transformation requires one step at a time. I hope you can accept exactly where you are, and at the same time, look forward to where you are going. Now back to Susan before we move on to the next step of putting all of this into action.

As I did with many of my clients, Susan and I started focusing and working on one thing (one behavior, habit, or practice) that was identified in the start, stop, and continue exercise while both of us fully understood there were bigger and deeper things we needed to explore and shift. Because we are all on our own journey, we have to allow ourselves to "go there" only when we are ready. This is the next mountain Susan and I had to climb together.

As we made progress on the work front, Susan began to share some challenges in her personal life. She was working all the time and had little time, let alone energy, left in the tank for her family, and she made absolutely no time for herself. She was carrying guilt and experiencing some health challenges. I was honored and grateful she trusted me enough to explore these things with her, and I let her know how brave she was for bringing this up.

None of us likes to face our struggles. We don't like to feel vulnerable, and we fear appearing weak. We don't want to risk being judged or admit to ourselves that in some way we have failed because we didn't make better choices. I get it. I have felt these things over and over, as I've worked through my own restoration process. The most beautiful part of this healing and realignment process is that you learn to let go of those feelings and redirect your energy into acceptance and moving forward. We are all just doing the best we can, and we will continue to learn new and better ways, and when we know better, we can do better. It's as simple as that.

It was perfectly clear to both of us how Susan got here. There was no shame in it and no reason to dwell on it. We just needed to sit with the reality of where we were and decide what we would do about it. As we discussed possible starting points and small steps, there was hesitation in her demeanor, resistance to the suggestions we were exploring. She was nodding her head about some options, but I could tell she wasn't convinced.

I pointed out my observations around this and opened space for us to lean into the resistance. There was some natural "I've tried this before" processing that occurred, but I could tell that there was something deeper. I asked her if she believed she deserved to put herself first. That question clearly hit a nerve. She understood why her health and time to herself were important, but she held on to a belief that anything she did just for her was selfish. This is a very common belief among women, especially mothers.

Instead of arguing with her about whether or not it was selfish, I asked her to explain her perspective and offered some alternatives. If we couldn't get her mind and heart changed about this, there was little hope for us being successful in pursuing any action. See how these things are tied together? As we move toward action, we may get stuck in several places. Lean into the resistance and allow yourself to be in it and work through it until it shifts versus forcing yourself into something that you will resist and because of that, will likely not persist.

Eventually Susan got past feeling like she was being selfish. It took us a good thirty-five minutes to process together and some continued focus on affirmations. We decided to just work on that instead of taking an actual step between that session and our next one. She showed up to our next session convinced and even excited to take a step, and she had given herself time to discern and decide which one would be best for her.

Staying present and aware as we move toward action is imperative to be successful. Progress is not always linear, and sometimes, we have to allow ourselves to back up and work through things, sidestep and explore, or even take a time out. When we are digging up the roots of what has always been and essentially changing the foundation, patience is required. There is no quick fix or silver bullet. Allow yourself the space to work through determining what needs to change. If you haven't allowed space to do this or created deep discernment for these things, then the next step of developing your action plan will be irrelevant. You will not have the right things on your plan or in the right order.

TWO SIMPLE PRACTICES THAT CAN PROFOUNDLY CHANGE YOU AND YOUR LIFE

Before I take you into building your action plan, I'd like to take you deeper into one of the most impactful things you can do to become your best self and reach your fullest potential: developing morning and evening routines. As you may recall, in Chapter 4, we established some understanding around your morning and evening routines or lack thereof. We narrowed in on one thing you could do to positively evolve that routine. Here, we will explore your morning and evening routine more holistically and give you a framework to more intentionally develop yours to support who you want to become.

Each day is a gift filled with incredible opportunities for transformation, but only if you are intentional about each of them. This is a tall task, because as humans, we are wired to fall into autopilot and just buzz through the days, only to "wake up" years later wondering where our time went.

Earlier in the book, I said the first step in becoming your best self is connection. Establishing morning and evening routines systematizes and wires connection into our day. We can put simple practices in place that will make a profound difference over time.

My morning and evening routines have changed me. I was recently having lunch with a friend and former coworker. She asked me to share my secret with her. I asked, "What secret is that?" She replied, "How do you stay so calm and confident amid all that is happening in the world?" My answer to her was simple, "I stick to my morning and evening routines consistently, no matter what. They help me stay rooted, regardless of what I face and keep me coming back to the Way, the Truth, and the Life."

I shared with her what my morning routine looked like, and as I continued talking, I could see her start to squirm. She asked, "You do all that? Every day of the week?" This is the typical response I get when sharing my routine with someone for the first time. I had to remind her that this routine, in its current form, was developed over a span of years. I started with one small thing and kept stacking and adding things to it that felt good for me. I hope you will do the same as you consider adding it to your action plan. Pick one thing and stick with it until you have it mastered and integrated it, then add to your routine bit by bit.

Developing a Morning Routine

If you choose to be more intentional about the beginning of your day, consider the following options as soon as you open your eyes, before you do anything else and before your to-do list starts scrolling in your mind:

- Say thank you for being alive.
- Think about three things you are grateful for.
- Take five deep, cleansing breaths.

Notice how this makes you feel. Part of creating positive change is reflecting on and creating awareness around the shifts in your energy. You will stick to it if you can see and feel the changes, but you need to make space for that to happen. This starts with you simply becoming more present and aware. This consciousness is the foundation upon which you can build joy and peace. It fosters calm and courage. It is simple but difficult to be disciplined about. Start here and make one or all three of these consciousness practices part of your morning routine. As these become a habit, you can start to layer more things into your morning routine that help you come into your day as your best self. Here are some suggestions:

- Spend a few minutes in the silence and stillness.
- Take two to five minutes for meditation and/or prayer.
- Read a devotional.
- Read the Bible or another book of wisdom.
- Listen to a podcast.
- Take time to read.
- Spend a few minutes journaling.
- Move your body in some way (yoga, walking, weight lifting, etc.).
- Create and say some positive affirmations.
- Make your bed.
- Take a couple of minutes to think about who you want to be today and set an intention.

The mornings are a great time to invest in yourself and get what you need for the day. If we can focus on ourselves first and fill up with the love and positive energy we need, then we will have it to give. For many of us, when the house starts waking up, we lose the chance to do what we need for us. Make and take this sacred time. It can make a world of difference in how you show up and how you feel.

Once you feel good about who you want to be and how you want to be, spend some time preparing for what you want to do. Most of us get swept up in our day the minute we open our computer, get to the office, or receive our first phone call, reacting to whatever comes our way. We get to the end of the day feeling like we didn't get anything accomplished.

To achieve something, we have to be clear about what it is we are setting out to do. Make time to think about or write down one to three things you need to get done that day in your personal life and for your family. This is especially important for individuals who feel like they are stretched and like they aren't doing well at work or at home. Doing the laundry, cooking dinner, taking out the trash, picking up the house—these are all very important duties to create a safe and loving environment for our families, but we don't count them as productive. These fundamental duties are so important for the health and well-being of you and your family. They count. Wake up when you are doing them, and do them with care and love. Friend, you don't need to do more, you just need to do what you're doing with more awareness, intention, and love.

As you are ready, consider doing the same at work. What are one to three things you need to prioritize for yourself and get done today? This is an especially important exercise for leaders and those who manage people. If you want to be fully present to the needs of your team and excel in your role, you need to be very intentional about where you spend your time and energy. Take the first five to ten minutes of your day to make your list and figure out where in your day you can get these things done. Maybe you need to come in thirty minutes early. Maybe you need to close your door or find a place where you can work for a period of time uninterrupted. Make it happen.

Look at your list. Is it filled with only things to "check off the list"? What about spending time with your people? What about communicating vision and checking in on performance? What about time to think strategically about the future? Think innovatively about how you could do things better. We fill our calendars so full of to-dos that we miss great opportunities to connect, innovate, learn, and grow. Don't get so caught up in the doing that you forget the most important part—having time to think and time to connect and create alignment. Investing in these things up front will help you avoid a lot of headache now and down the road.

Developing an Evening Routine

The evening gives us a great opportunity to learn, grow, and let go if we make space for reflection. We start our day with goals, plans, assumptions, and expectations . . . and then the day happens. Instead of making space to let go, learn, and grow, we rush into the next thing we need to do. If it was a frustrating day, we bring that energy into our home and the evening's activities. There is another way. A more intentional one.

To start, consider building in five to ten minutes at the end of your workday for wrap up, reflection, and planning. Ask yourself:

- What went well today?
- What did I check off my list?
- What was challenging today?
- What do I need to let go of from the day?

Take a look at these questions. I hope you notice a pattern because it is one you can carry into every situation of your life after it unfolds. These are great questions to incorporate into our everyday life, so we can become aware, celebrate, learn, let go, grow, and be more intentional!

- "What went well today?" forces you to take inventory of your day and become consciously aware of the positive things that happened. Even on the toughest days, there are small things we can recognize as good if we are disciplined enough to look.

- "What did I check off my list?" helps you become aware of whether you are putting first things first, or maybe even aware of the fact that you don't yet have a list and you are simply reacting and responding to anything that comes at you. With so many distractions, so much noise, and so many demands, it takes real focus and discipline to take hold of our lives and what is ours to do. This question brings us to the reality of our discipline and focus and gives us a chance to see what things we may have checked off that weren't originally on our radar. There are days where we have to set aside things on our list for unexpected issues and opportunities. Becoming aware of that too and celebrating the good, important work we do in those unexpected moments is a path to growth as well. Having a plan and staying open to new opportunities or adjusting course is a skill we should aim to master as a leader.

- "What was challenging today?" helps you face what you typically avoid. These are the situations we play over and over in our heads at the dinner table. These are the stories that cause us anxiety. These are the feelings we avoid by keeping ourselves busy or numbing out. When we have the courage to face this question, a whole new set of learning opportunities present themselves. Life is challenging, unpredictable, and often uncomfortable. When we believe that everything should be good and easy, we set ourselves up for disappointment, anxiety, and frustration. When we avoid the truth to this question and push away our feelings, we keep ourselves prisoner to the way things are instead of considering what could be and how we could create positive change.

- "What do I need to let go of from the day?" is the next practical and productive question if you are willing to ask yourself "What was challenging today?" The fact is that many of the challenging things we face are outside of our control, yet we do everything we can to try and control them. We hold on to them in our heads and hearts, which creates anxiety. We try to force things instead of allowing them to unfold. We work to control other people even. As you evaluate your answers to what was challenging, think about what was really within your control?

When I started my own journey, I was in sales, and I would replay over and over the sales calls I had that didn't go well. I would spend copious amounts of time and energy shaming myself for what I could have done better and wishing I had another chance. One day, my mentor pointed out that the shaming was actually damaging my ability to be effective in the opportunities I currently had and that I had an opportunity to correct some of my said "mistakes" from the calls I was stewing over simply by taking action.

He said, "If you forgot to ask a question you needed an answer for in the discovery, simply call or email them back with the question instead of spending all this energy beating yourself up that you didn't the first time. If you believe there was something more you could have said or done, say or do it now."

These were simple concepts and yet so revelatory to me. You mean I don't have to beat myself up, *and* I can take action to change the situation?! It was the simplest shift from the past to the present: Let go of what was, and focus on what could be. This totally changed my life and my approach.

Several of the sales I thought were dead, I picked right back up and took to the finish line as a result. Whatever had transpired wasn't an ending. Pretty soon, I was in pursuit of the first "no" I could get because I knew it was one hurdle in the pursuit of helping them understand how I could help them and why they needed the solution I had. I took all that energy I was wasting on the past, shifted it into the present, and acted on the lessons I'd learned to create a positive future.

As you are ready, consider building in a small evening routine that helps you transition into bedtime and sleep. Try some of these suggestions:

- **Create awareness**—How are you feeling? What are you thinking about?

- **Release tension**—Think about what you need to forgive yourself for. Make a list and release it.

- **Shift your focus**—Consider three things you are grateful for from your day.

- **Celebrate**—Identify one thing you appreciate about yourself from the day or one thing you did well.

- **Set an intention or read a devotional.**

Start with the first one and work your way down through the list over time. Creating awareness alone can be a very powerful step. As you then move into shifting your focus, you can start to see small joys amid even the most stressful of days. Each day, even the most mundane one, offers you an opportunity to learn something new or serve someone. It's all about your perspective. You'll start to see all the things you *get* to do instead of all the things you *have* to do.

During our time together in this chapter, we have determined what needs to change from the inside out. Our internal transformation can drive external change, and external change can drive internal transformation. We want to provide space for all of that to help us embrace and live out the best version of ourselves. Don't underestimate the impact that small tweaks can make, especially over time.

REFLECT ON YOUR JOURNEY

- What have you learned, unlearned, or relearned in this chapter?

- What has been most valuable to you?

- What one thing will you commit to doing differently going forward?

- Who can you invite in to keep you accountable?

CHAPTER 13

Developing an Action Plan

We all like to dream and talk about our plans, but most of us don't appreciate the discipline it takes to get that plan down into something that can be managed and measured. Doing so can feel constricting and, at times, like it takes the fun out of the entire process. Trust me, I know. But I have come to appreciate the freedom I have found in having a framework. I put in the work to get my action plan down on paper, and now all I have to do is take action and reflect on my progress. Having an action plan is a great source of accountability and celebration if you put in the work to do it. Let's follow along again with my client Susan, this time to learn the steps for developing an action plan.

Susan had previously identified and actually made some of the heart and mindset shifts to be successful in taking the next step, so she was ready to put those things into a sequence that was clear, actionable, and timebound.

As part of the work to develop actionable items, Susan and I used the start, stop, and continue method to identify key themes related to her behaviors, practices, and routines/habits. (Susan made her own list and then invited her friends, family, and colleagues to share their thoughts too.) Here are the themes she compiled:

- Start prioritizing yourself and your family.
- Start investing in your health and longevity.
- Start delegating.
- Stop saying yes to everything that comes your way.
- Stop dwelling on mistakes or past decisions.
- Stop taking on what is not the highest and best use of your time.
- Continue caring about and for others.
- Continue creating and communicating your vision.
- Continue letting your guard down.

Once we had this list on paper, we discussed which items felt the most true and important and how we could put them into an action plan. First, Susan needed to be firmly rooted in why she would make a change and to know that all of this effort would have purpose and meaning. She also needed something that could point her back to her plan when she wavered, and bring her back up when she was feeling down or defeated. That "something" is the purpose statement of the action plan. If you remember, Susan felt selfish putting herself and her needs first because of how she had been conditioned. It was important to word her purpose statement in a way that felt good and true to her heart and in a way that motivated and inspired her to move forward in the difficult moments.

We landed on this for Susan's purpose statement: *I prioritize my needs and invest in my longevity, so I can maximize time with my family and my impact on the world.*

Once we had a purpose statement that felt good and right, we could move on to what would be different. In business, we often call these success statements, and for individual clients, I like to use the term *New Truths*. These paint a picture for what we are trying to accomplish and what good/done/success looks like. Susan developed three New Truths:

1. I prioritize quality time with my family.

2. My health markers are in a good place.

3. My yeses will be used only for things that maximize my gifts, calling, and contributions.

Susan and I would be using these New Truths to build an action plan between where she was and the steps she needed to take to make them true.

We also needed to outline her nonnegotiables—these are commitments that align to our New Truths and can serve as a checkpoint for us to know whether we are on or off track. In the midst of change and transformation, things get messy. We can get lost in the struggle and in all that is changing and not changing. Confusion and frustration can set in. We won't meet all of our milestones and goals. The nonnegotiables serve as a solid foundation that we can come back to and show us that we are winning and making progress. They are lead indicators and the actions we must take to ensure we will get the outcomes we are hoping for as we make progress. It can be easiest if you start with one New Truth and develop nonnegotiables related to that truth, then move on to the next New Truth and a new set of nonnegotiables, and so on.

Susan named three nonnegotiables related to her first New Truth, *I prioritize quality time with my family*:

1. Eat dinner with my family at least three nights per week.

2. Prioritize and plan family vacations.

3. Attend and be fully present at family events and activities.

Susan is an influential leader with a big job and many commitments. Bringing her back to these nonnegotiables uncomplicates things and helps her think differently about her responsibilities and what success looks like. In previous versions of herself, she was so focused on her work that everything else simply got the leftovers. By committing to thinking and acting differently, Susan will live differently. Let's move on to the action steps.

The action steps fill the gap between where we are and where we want to be. Some people may need to go back to heart and mindset shifts. Maybe your first step is saying an affirmation or repeating your purpose statement until your heart and mind believe that what you are saying and attempting to do is or can be true. Some people have a hard time figuring out what the steps could be between where they are and where they want to be. That's OK and totally normal! You are in your life, and sometimes an outside perspective is all that is needed to see the steps. If you get stuck at any point, invite someone else in to help you in this process.

For Susan's first New Truth—*I prioritize quality time with my family*—to be true and to meet her first nonnegotiable—*Eat dinner with my family at least three nights a week*, we developed the following action steps. Note that Susan's heart and mind were already convinced of these things, so those shifts didn't need to be made; she just needed to take different action. Also note that many of the action steps we developed for her first New Truth and first nonnegotiable also helped the second and third nonnegotiables to be true. Sometimes it happens this way and sometimes it doesn't, but when there is overlap, it's fewer action steps for you to take, so work to find the common action steps that support all of your nonnegotiables.

Step 1 of the action plan was a review of Susan's calendar and work habits: When did she start and end work? What type of work was coming in and how? What were her response habits? What was taking up most of her time? What were the things that only she could do? It is always important to start with an assessment or review so you know the facts of what you are dealing with.

We did a full audit of her current situation to uncover habits that could be improved and to see what could be delegated. Susan is quick, thoughtful, and thorough, so the only way we could solve for her issues and create more time for her family, friends, and herself would be to improve systems and shift work to others.

Step 2 was implementing a couple (yes, just a couple) of changes we thought would be most impactful. These included creating more white space (remember in Chapter 8 we defined white space as time to invest in care; to process, think, and discern; to reset and regroup; to pray; etc.) in her calendar for contemplation and deep work, and to give space for follow up, checking email, and the unexpected interruptions that happened every day. We decided to leave 8:00–10:00 a.m. and 4:00–5:00 p.m. open every day and schedule one hour of deep-work time. With her schedule being so full, we did what we could to shift things immediately but had to wait eight full weeks before we could plan and try out the new schedule.

White space and margin (time between meetings and between activities) are things I see as issues for almost every leader I work with. They're issues I battle as well. To do our best and highest-value work, we need white space—time to think about the work we are doing, time to plan, time to think through things, time to execute well, and time to reflect and learn. It's hard to justify "think and plan time" when we have so much to do, but how do we know we are working on the right things if we aren't thinking about what we are working on?

Add to this dilemma that as leaders, we are high achievers and want to maximize our time, so we fill our schedules with things that need to get done. The trouble is that work and life are unpredictable. We get interrupted, things come in that we weren't expecting, we have to support someone else, and pretty soon, we are working through our lunch, coming in early, and working late. If we want to honor some semblance of a life outside of work, we must force ourselves to be reasonable and realistic about how many hours in a day can be scheduled and how many hours we need to leave open to respond to the unexpected. We do this by creating margin. This amount of time will vary based on the type of role you have.

In addition to creating margin in her schedule, Susan and I determined that for Step 3 she needed to build in some longer-term strategies, such as having someone help her with triaging emails, so we made a plan for delegation. This plan included what would need to be in place for the task to be handed off (training, a conversation, a checklist, etc.) and who would take it by when.

For Step 4, we audited Susan's personal life and relationships to assess their impact and create action around those. I asked her to consider everything she was currently committed to outside of her immediate family activities, and we started to identify what she felt obligated to do versus what she felt motivated to do. We did the same thing with her list of friends and family. Who was she motivated to spend time with and develop deeper relationships with and who did she feel obligated to do those things with? It's amazing how quickly our time gets filled with people who want to spend time with us, but we may not desire to spend time with them. Susan was a great listener, so she had a lot of friends who called her for advice and support but did not reciprocate that with her. We had to consider how we might create some space in these relationships, so she felt energized and excited to see them.

Now that we had Susan's action steps outlined, we could put them into a template where we could also see her purpose statement, New

Truths, and nonnegotiables. This allowed us to check in on the action steps, while at the same time seeing if she was meeting her nonnegotiables and identifying what progress she was making toward her New Truths. This seems like a lot of work for goal-setting and tracking, but if we don't put in the work to be specific and make it simple, it's almost certain we won't follow through. The following framework outlines the action plan for Susan that includes her purpose statement, New Truths, nonnegotiables, and action steps.

Purpose Statement: I prioritize my needs and invest in my longevity, so I can maximize time with my family and my impact on the world.

New Truths:

1. I prioritize quality time with my family.
2. My health markers are in a good place.
3. My yeses will be used only for things that maximize my gifts, calling, and contributions.

Nonnegotiables for New Truth 1:

1. Eat dinner with my family at least three nights per week.
2. Prioritize and plan family vacations.
3. Attend and be fully present at family events and activities.

Action Steps for New Truth 1 and Nonnegotiables:

Step 1: Review and Assess Calendar and Work Habits

1. Perform review of my calendar and work habits and identify what needs to change by [date].

Step 2: Implement Immediate and Impactful Changes

1. Calendar daily white space time (8:00–10:00 a.m. and 4:00–5:00 p.m.).

2. Calendar deep-work time (one hour per day).

Step 3: Build Action Steps for Longer-Term Strategies

1. Identify person to triage email and build email triage plan and parameters.

2. Implement email triage plan and checkpoints to review and adjust.

3. Identify all tasks that can be handed off as well as people and plans for handoffs.

4. Execute handoffs and schedule check-ins for any necessary adjustments.

Step 4: Assess Other Impacts and Create Action

1. Audit personal commitments.

2. Identify personal commitments to eliminate and build plan to adjust.

3. Identify personal relationship priorities.

4. Identify commitments needed in order to spend time with those on the priority list.

Now that you see the pattern, I hope you can interpret how to determine the nonnegotiables and action plans for the rest of the New Truths. You'll note that in the Susan example, I did not address timelines, but they are a critical part of the process. On the template shown, you'll see a space to insert a date in the first action step—and dates should be added to each step. Our intentions and commitments fail when we aren't specific enough about what needs to be done and when we don't put deadlines or timelines in place. To ensure these commitments are more likely to stick, I like talking with my clients up front about the consequences of not following through.

If we leave it simply as an "oh well," or we allow excuses to get in our way with no consequences, most of us will not have the accountability to follow through. Sheer willpower only gets us so far. The consequences don't have to be negative, but they do need to incentivize you to be serious about prioritizing your commitments and sticking to the timelines.

Susan chose to pick a consequence that aligned with her health goals, which was actually a win-win for her in the grand scheme of things. For every deadline that she missed on the plan, she had to walk an extra fifteen minutes. She also used that same consequence to address not sticking to her commitment of daily white space and deep-work time. Susan had a tight schedule, so the idea of trying to fit in even more exercise (this was also not something she really enjoyed) was an incentive—*and* if it had to be enforced, it aligned with some of her other goals.

You may not find a win-win like that, but if you can, that's great! Other examples of consequences that can be used as incentives while also being beneficial include skipping a meal, spending time in silence and solitude/meditation/prayer, reading or listening to a book, journaling or writing, handwriting a note to someone, going to an extra church service, not eating out for a week, engaging in an activity related to pure enjoyment or play (for me, it's swinging on the swings at the park), doing an extra workout, and drinking coffee from home versus your favorite coffee shop. Again, these are incentives because they force us to slow down—and none of us feels we have the time to do that—but they also greatly benefit our lives in different ways. Consider what other meaningful tasks you don't make time for, what things you avoid that are actually good for you, or what "conveniences" make you too comfortable or cost you money.

Now that I've helped you see what creating an action plan looks like through an example, let's give you some space to think about your own purpose statement, New Truths, nonnegotiables, and action plan.

YOUR ACTION PLAN

Your purpose statement is the north star to everything else that you will develop. It tells you your *why* and what success looks like, and your New Truths, nonnegotiables, and action plan should all align to and drive toward it. I find it helpful to develop the New Truths, nonnegotiables, and action plan and then come back to the purpose statement, but do this in the order that works for you. The following exercises include some additional questions and pointers to help you develop these things for your own journey.

YOUR NEW TRUTHS

To discover your New Truths, consider the following questions about what you want to change. The purpose of the first question is to get you to consider what needs to change. The second question forces you to identify how you will measure progress or success—it focuses on outcomes. When my clients set goals, they often focus on the input and the action they will take, but sometimes that won't get them the result they want. By focusing on the outcome or result, you can adjust your approach to ensure you get to where you want to go. Ask yourself:

- What will be different?
- How will you know you've arrived or are successful?

YOUR NONNEGOTIABLES

There are priorities, values, and other things that you need to keep in mind if you don't want them to be sacrificed or compromised in this process of change. Consider those good parts of you and your life that you don't want to lose sight of—the following two questions can help you face your trade-offs honestly and honor those things.

For instance, Susan was determined to find time in her day to exercise, but one of her nonnegotiables was dinner with her family, so this forced her to think about how she would fit her exercise in without compromising that time. When you don't face these trade-offs and name your nonnegotiables, you can end up violating or compromising on something that leaves you worse off than before. To identify your nonnegotiables, ask yourself:

- What cannot change?
- What must be in place for your New Truths to become true?

YOUR ACTION PLAN

The hardest part of building an action plan for many people is taking everything they've outlined and putting it into actionable steps with timelines, so they can make and measure progress. You have to bring everything from theory into reality. This is a gift that comes to some very naturally, so if you are stuck on getting the New Truths broken down into action steps, invite someone to help you do that.

You also need to be honest with yourself about what's reasonable and realistic when outlining these steps. If you desire to be a more positive person, and today you are a negative Nancy, jumping straight from where you are into providing praise and compliments to others is not reasonable. A good first step might be to identify the negative thoughts with no initial intention of changing them. This first step is simply to become aware of your negative thoughts. A next step might be to catch the thought and choose not to react or respond. Where you may have said something negative out loud as a result of your thought before, you simply bite your tongue. That is progress and a reasonable next step. You can keep building on that until you arrive at giving praise and compliments. Small and consistent action that is sustainable will have a much bigger impact over time. As you build your action plan, ask yourself:

- What are the gaps between where you are and where you want to be?

- What are the steps to make those shifts?

The complex part of putting all of these things into an action plan is that, while we do need to put some stakes in the ground and make commitments, we must also keep an open mind and open heart that the plan may need to change. We are learning through this process, and we can't know everything going in. We need to commit, so we can make forward progress but be intentional about regrouping and reorienting as needed. If you are trying something and it isn't working, give yourself space to evaluate why and to try other things. When we stick to the plan at all costs, we often end up in a failed plan. We have to be adaptable and flexible in reaching the end result.

Another thing to note: Plans often fail because they aren't clear and specific enough, they don't have timelines, or they aren't visible. I am offering ideas that I have used myself and with other clients to ensure plans are clear and specific, timebound, and visible, but you have to take responsibility to make this plan your own and create a system and structure that works for you and your life.

Your High-Level Plan

Start with a high-level, one-page plan like this one:

My Action Plan Template

> **Purpose Statement:** Write one sentence that captures the *why* behind your action plan and the essence of the changes and impact you would like to see.

> **New Truths:** List two to three truths that will exist if you are living out your purpose statement and action plan. What will be different? How will you know you are successful? These should be measurable in some way.

> **Nonnegotiables:** List the things that you cannot compromise on as you undertake this action plan. These are important

things in your life that you cannot lose sight of or must remain the same. If it's helpful and easier, write out nonnegotiables for each New Truth.

Action Steps:

List all of the steps here for you to get from where you are today to your New Truths. Depending on how detailed you want to be, you can document each step and milestone, or you can simply list the highlights. These action steps should be clear and thorough enough that you can easily stay on track to achieve your New Truths and live out your purpose without losing sight of your nonnegotiables.

You can use this template to develop your life plan, a leadership plan, or any other kind of personal plan.

Breaking Down the Steps

Take the action steps and break them down even further, if needed. Then add them to your calendar, your to-do list, or whatever other system you use to manage your priorities. For example, the first action step on Susan's action plan is: *Perform review of my calendar and work habits by [date]*. Here is how I would break that down further:

1. Review the calendar and identify things like the top three tasks or activities that are taking up the most time. Ask these questions:

   · What tasks or activities could be eliminated or delegated?

   · What tasks or activities are draining?

2. Consider your daily, weekly, and monthly habits, and evaluate:

- How am I planning and preparing for my days?

- How am I unwinding?

- When am I starting?

- When am I shutting down?

- How many breaks do I need to feel at my best?

- How much white space do I need to leave for things that pop up?

- When during the day and week am I most productive at what tasks?

- What time of day do I have the most energy and creativity?

- How do I keep myself accountable to commitments and following up?

- What issues do I encounter that could be addressed with better habits and what are those habits?

Susan figured out a few things, but these rose to the top as the most important to start with: 1) She was in several meetings she didn't need to be in; 2) She wasn't leaving enough space for things that popped up; she had about four hours a day of unanticipated issues she would have to address; 3) She was allowing emails and other urgent-but-not-important tasks to overtake her plans and schedule. Here's how we tackled the issues:

1. **She was in several meetings she didn't need to be in**—We put a plan in place for her to communicate to the owners of those meetings why she needed to drop out, and a deadline by which to get them off her calendar. We implemented criteria for her

to request going forward if someone wanted her to participate in a meeting to make sure it was the highest and best use of her time: purpose of the meeting, agenda, and the role they wanted her to play/value she would add.

2. **She wasn't leaving enough space for things that popped up—** We had to go out about eight weeks, but we picked a date by which she would allow for four hours of white space per day in her calendar. That time could get filled with these things that popped up, or if nothing popped up, she could work on something in her prioritized list of tasks and projects. This one change shifted her from working until 11:00 p.m. almost every night to having time to eat dinner with her family and staying off her computer at least three nights per week.

3. **She was allowing emails and other urgent-but-not-important tasks to overtake her plans and schedule—**We agreed to two designated times during the day when she would check her emails and a date by which she would start using that process. Ahead of that date, we told everyone that if they had something urgent, they needed to call or text. We also handed the triage of her emails off to someone else on a particular date, allowing many messages to be responded to without Susan reading or touching them. For the first time in her career, she came back from vacation with hardly anything in her mailbox and without the need to spend a whole day just catching up on emails. Big wins!

There is no right or wrong way to break down the action steps; the important thing is that you have enough detail that you can stay on track and know what to do next.

Get It Down on Paper

Following the examples and using the advice I have shared, go ahead and craft your action plan. Really take time with this part of the process. This is where the rubber meets the road. I love the saying "slow down to go fast" and it applies perfectly here. If we don't put enough time and effort into being clear and concise with our plan, timelines, and how success will be measured, we will severely limit our chances of positive change and lasting results.

This part of the book and our restoration process can feel tedious and time-consuming. Think about it; this is where most of us fall off the wagon with our plans. We've discovered and dreamed, and now we've got to be specific about what we will do differently. That takes commitment, willpower, and discipline. If you find yourself desiring to skimp on this step and skip forward, I challenge you to dig a little deeper. How you commit to this step—how you create your action plan—will drive and determine your success from here. Commit. You deserve it!

REFLECT ON YOUR JOURNEY

- What have you learned, unlearned, or relearned in this chapter?

- What has been most valuable to you?

- What one thing will you commit to doing differently going forward?

- Who can you invite in to keep you accountable?

CHAPTER 14

Receiving Support

Now that you have a plan on paper, it's time to share it. That's right, the next step is not to take action but to invite others into the plan with you. This is for several reasons: 1) You will need support and encouragement; 2) accountability with another person makes us more likely to stick to our commitments; and 3) gaining other perspectives on how you could execute the action steps or what might trip you up will strengthen your plan.

As I've said time and time again, we can't do life alone. We need each other if we want to reach our potential! One of the most radical acts of self-care is to allow others to love, support, and help us. This will be uncomfortable for many of us because we don't know how to let others in. Let's look at a couple of concepts that can help you in this process.

CHOOSE YOUR SUPPORT SYSTEM CAREFULLY

When asking for support, consider who you need and who you trust. By need, I mean, you will need a cheerleader and a challenger—someone to celebrate the progress and someone to point out when you are off course. Sometimes those are the same person, but often they are two different people. Most of us don't enjoy being challenged, so when you can be clear with someone that their role is precisely to challenge you, it can create a more positive dynamic as you go through this journey together.

We also need people willing to process with us as things shift and change—who we trust to provide wise counsel when we need to pivot. I have found, in my own journey, that people who have walked a similar path or have more life experience are very helpful in this arena. They might not be as close to me, which is also a gift, because they see me and the situation with new eyes and a fresh perspective.

An additional thing to consider is whether you engage friendly support or paid support. What we are asking of others, even the cheerleader, requires firm commitment. Sometimes inviting our friends or family members into these situations can put extra strain on the relationship, and we need to be mindful of that.

I like to keep my friends and family members informed, but I do not like to put the full burden of being my ally and confidant in the journey on them. I prefer to pay for coaches, healers, and counselors and engage with other professionals like spiritual directors and mentors where there is a more explicit intent for our relationship, so that with my friends and family members, we can be just that—friends and family.

I might share my intentions and plans with friends and family at a high level and share progress and struggles, but I am not actively processing during our time together. For me, this separation has brought a lot of freedom and peace to my personal relationships. It allows me to be fully open and honest with my designated and paid allies and confidants, while sharing with friends and family in a way that is not burdensome.

SHARE WITH INTENTION

I have learned this the hard way by being both roles in the journey. Early in my marriage, I was putting the full burden of everything I was experiencing in life and work on my husband by using our evenings together to process and problem-solve. This is very common in marriages and can add a ton of additional stress. Yes, we want to share with our partners and be in it together, but the reality is that no one person should carry that load with you on their own. We need multiple baskets to put our emotional eggs in.

The same thing happens in friendships. One person uses the relationship to process all their stuff, so the other person rarely gets the chance to share in return, with the result that it no longer feels like a mutual relationship. Encounters like these are draining. Sometimes this happens when someone is going through a hard season, but usually people unknowingly create a pattern and relationship dynamic that doesn't feel great. You need to be aware of this because you don't want to be that person, and so put boundaries in place where needed.

LEADERSHIP'S ROLE IN SUPPORTING PERSONAL CHALLENGES AND GROWTH

Many leaders feel the need to support team members who are struggling mentally and emotionally. But this support usually comes on top of a full plate of daily work responsibilities. I'm not saying this is right or wrong; I'm simply asking you to consider from the perspective of being a leader what is reasonable and realistic for you and those around you when it comes to all of these expectations.

Most leaders I know do not have the capacity or the capability to meet the needs of their employees when it comes to their mental and emotional health. While we as leaders don't want to discourage people from feeling safe to show up openly and honestly at work, we do want to encourage them to take responsibility for showing up healthy and whole. The workplace is not where we should be bringing our personal issues in to process. It is our responsibility to find resources outside of work time (and probably work people) to do that, so we can show up ready to do the work we collectively need to get done. As leaders, we can offer resources and ideas, but it is the individual's responsibility to get the support and help they need. We need to be committed to modeling this, so that our employees are encouraged to do it too.

Many people are struggling with more than just situational struggles or circumstantial challenges. Many of them don't have the emotional language or coping skills to name or manage what they are facing. In these cases, we as leaders need to provide resources and encourage and empower people to increase their self-awareness, emotional intelligence, and overall well-being. Too often, I see leaders take the power out of the hands of their team members by overhelping or stepping in as the emotional support system.

In an ideal scenario, leaders have created an environment where employees can talk openly about personal struggles (because they do affect us and the way we work) and then have resources available so employees can take the steps they need to get to a healthy and whole place. As leaders, we need these resources too. All of us need support, ideas, resources, and accountability to become our best as a human. Without that baseline, nothing else will stick for the long term in our growth and development.

Here is a peek into what that looks like for me in my business. My teammates and I at The Restoration Project were friends long before we started working together. But we also all worked in the coaching and development field. This naturally created a dynamic where we would cross personal and professional lines often, meaning that we would talk about work when out for fun, and we would find ourselves processing our personal stuff in a work meeting. This wasn't healthy for us or productive for our business.

CREATING A COLLECTIVE VISION OF HOW WE WANT THINGS TO LOOK AND FEEL

Before my teammates and I could address the logistics to make this work for us, we first had to get aligned on our collective vision. We had to decide what we wanted our business and working together to look and feel like and the same for our friendship and time outside of work. This is a significant and often-overlooked step in all of our relationships. We need to define what *good* looks and feels like, as well as what's OK and what's not OK.

We agreed that outside of work, we would hold each other accountable to not talking about work. When someone brought up work, we would have fun in reminding them that we could save that for our next team meeting or within the hours of eight and five. Let's be honest, it was usually me breaking the rule, and I needed accountability to not drag others back into work when they were ready to be done with it for the day!

Inside of eight to five, we agreed that we wanted everyone to be open to how they were really feeling and not have to try and hide anything. We wanted it to feel safe to be who and how we really were, *and* we agreed that in our meetings and with each other was not the space to process what we were struggling with. That needed to be reserved for outside of business hours and with other people, like our own coaches, therapists, or healers. Our ultimate goal was that each of us had the support systems in place to show up healthy and whole to work together. That's what we strive for each and every day.

Now, let's talk about what that looks like in practical and tactical terms. First, when one of us asks how the others are doing, we share honestly how we are feeling in a succinct manner. "I'm struggling today," "I have a short fuse today," or "I'm feeling great today" are perfectly good answers. If someone is interested in learning more about what that means, they can go and ask, but we each have a responsibility not to put what's happening energetically or otherwise on the other team members, because it's not just about one of us as an individual, it's about all of us as a whole.

Second, we create containers—intentional and safe spaces—in our weekly meetings with the whole team for each of us to share our highs and lows, or we use what we call a "transparency tidbit," which allows people to briefly share something important that's going on in their life right now, so we can stay connected and engaged at a human level. The purpose of this is to continue to grow our relationships and understand each other better, while not getting into all the nitty-gritty during the meeting. Once again, each person is welcome to ask for more details as they'd like on their own time.

Finally, once per quarter (and more often in a less formal manner, if desired), we conduct a deeper dive on how each team member is feeling about life and work, where they are aligned and misaligned with our core values, what they are learning, and how they are growing and developing in line with their plans and intentions. This is done off-site in a "celebration" format where we review the previous quarter's performance and more, then allow space for each team member to reflect, reset, and renew their commitment for the next quarter.

These quarterly celebrations have led to some of the most meaningful, insightful, innovative, and memorable conversations and moments we have had as a team and company. We are reminded of the progress we have made, the impact of the work we are doing, the fun we are having, the challenges we have faced and overcome, and how much we've grown, *and* we feel reconnected and recommitted to each other and the work we get to do together. This is the power of being in a community with others and receiving support in our dreams, goals, and plans.

BENEFITS OF INVITING OTHERS IN AND RECEIVING SUPPORT

There are a few other benefits of receiving support and inviting others in that I want to highlight. The process itself helps us grow as a person and as a leader. Overall, receiving support proves to us the power of collaboration. We have all heard the saying "two heads are better than one." But do we really believe that? In our culture today, we are pressured to figure everything out on our own and to go it alone. Most of us no longer believe in the power of collaboration, have never experienced it, or don't know how to do it.

Receiving support teaches us how to collaborate. Collaboration is defined as the action of working with someone to do something. I hold a deep belief that we should rarely go it alone. Anything worth doing is worth inviting someone else into, so they can help make it better. But how do we invite someone in to work *with*? Most of us know how to do things *for* or *to* people, but not *with*.

With requires allowance and acceptance. You have your way, they have their way, and now we must find a third way. The third way allows each person to show up with their own ideas and perspectives and experiences. It honors that those ways are true to that person. The third way requires refinement, clarity, and new ways of thinking and doing. It accepts an equal exchange of ideas and energy between both parties.

Receiving support teaches us humility. It requires acknowledgment that we don't have all the answers and we don't want to do this alone. That level of vulnerability is strong and courageous. It takes real guts to start the conversation and extend an invitation into your personal and professional journey.

The first step in humbling ourselves is to overcome our ego, which tells us we have all the answers and don't need anyone else. Then we have to overcome our fear of being perceived as weak or dumb because we don't "know it all." Spoiler alert: No one does! It's no wonder so many of us choose to keep our growth and development to ourselves. To this day, and in my most trusted relationships, I still find myself getting defensive and feeling the fear of someone thinking I'm not good enough. This may be the greatest hurdle to overcome and require the most strength, but it will not be the last challenge we face when receiving support.

Receiving support teaches us how to receive. Sounds obvious and basic, but as someone whose "One Word" was *receive* for a whole year, I can tell you that living this word is so much more complex than you can imagine. There are many definitions of *receive*, but my favorite is "to permit to enter." (Remember, in Chapter 9 we learned about the One Word practice where you focus on one word for the year and allow it to teach and transform you.)

It's one thing to invite someone into our story and to allow their support, encouragement, and ideas to be heard, but it's a whole other thing to actually *receive* them—to open ourselves up and allow them into our hearts and our minds. Don't let me lose you here; lean in with me!

How do you know if you are letting someone in and actually receiving them? Consider when you receive a compliment. When that compliment comes your way, what is your initial reaction? If you are like most people, your initial reaction is to explain it away, shrug it off, or even change the subject. We can be so uncomfortable with how vulnerable it feels to receive, that we will do anything to avoid it.

Now consider what it would look and feel like if you allowed that compliment to come your way, you looked the giver in the eyes and said thank you, and you put your hand over your heart, really allowing the words and the energy behind those words to sit in your heart for a while. Whoa—that's a significant difference!

We do the same thing with feedback and ideas. They are put in front of us, and we have to choose to receive them and allow them into our mind or to shut them out or down. This gets especially challenging when an idea is put in front of us that we don't agree with. Receiving that idea looks like taking it in, mulling it over, asking good questions, and really considering it. Receiving it doesn't mean that we agree, but it honors the gift that the other person has given us.

That takes me to the next skill that receiving support gives us, and that is the gift of *perspective taking*. We can begin to think that our way of seeing things is the only way, and that is dangerous ground. It's only in listening to and considering the experiences and perspectives of others that our beliefs and awareness become more refined.

OVERCOMING OUR FEAR OF OPPOSING VIEWS

There is a common misconception in the world today that the more you know and are exposed to, the more vulnerable you are to wrong thinking—becoming a victim to "evil" or straying from your morals. Based on my own lived experience and the teachings of some of the wisest people who have ever lived, there is little merit to this idea. Listening to and considering the perspectives of those who see things differently than we do, even perspectives directly opposed to the way we see things, can only improve our critical thinking if we are willing to leverage curiosity and discernment.

As you have likely picked up in my writing, I am a person of faith. I identify as a Christian. I was raised in a Christian family, and before I left for college, a family member implored me not to take any philosophy or anthropology classes in college because "the teachings in those classes directly contradict everything we believe."

What did I do? I immediately signed up for those classes. I was offended that this family member thought I was too dumb or too immature to think critically for myself. My experience in those classes was validation for all the questions I had carried with me but felt unable to ask. My classmates and I were all asking the same questions about life, death, identity, meaning, purpose, and justice.

The dialogue we engaged in as peers was accepting, expansive, and open, not dominating, limited, and closed, like I had experienced inside of my family or even my church. These conversations fed a desire in me to keep pursuing the truth and learning more. The same thing happened when I put myself in close relationship with people of different faiths and beliefs. Today, I have several close friends who have different beliefs than I do about several things, including religion. While we do not share the same beliefs, we do share a lot of the same values. Conversations with them are rich, inspiring, and challenging. They make me a better person and, if you can believe it, a better Christian.

To be in relationships with these friends, I had to get better at perspective taking. Perspective taking is not about believing or agreeing with whatever someone says to you, nor is it about shutting down whatever someone says that counters your belief. Instead, it requires providing a safe, open space for different voices, beliefs, perspectives, and experiences to be seen, heard, and understood.

When someone shares an opinion with me that, out of the gate, I feel conflicts with something I believe, I have two choices: remain open and allow that person to explain or shut it down and shut them up. If, as a human, I believe that every human on this planet has value (and this is a truth that many would agree with but have a hard time living out), then my only choice is to remain open. We have something to learn from every single person, and every living being (human and otherwise) deserves respect and care.

To take in different perspectives, we must create space by quieting our own voice. We must create relationships by investing time in care and connection. And we must create environments where we can exist together and share with each other well in advance of trying to solve a problem or take a stance. It is only when we allow other voices to be heard and alternatives to be considered that we can start to learn and then move toward improved, sustainable, worthy solutions.

Once we are able to open that space and receive other voices, we must employ discernment. Discernment is different from judgment. In the process of decision-making, discernment precedes judgment. We as people are not good at discernment because we typically skip straight to judgment.

Discernment is the quality of being able to grasp and comprehend what is obscure. It's about learning and considering, staying open to possibilities, rolling things around. *Judgment* is defined as the ability to make considered decisions or come to sensible conclusions. Can you see where we are going here?

Invite people in to collaborate	Take in perspectives	Practice discernment	Make a judgment or a call

I've found several practical ways to practice discernment:

1. Ask open-ended questions.
2. Invite more information.
3. Request that others provide their thoughts on the matter.
4. Give yourself space to process.
5. Research the subject.
6. Reflect and consider what was said against your own experience.

Discernment requires giving yourself the time and space to think critically and consider all sides. When you are able to hold two opposing views and truths and stand with your decision in a way that is calm and confident, not filled with extreme emotions, then you are likely in the right place and ready to move forward to making a judgment or a call. More and more of us need to give ourselves permission for more time for discernment.

We can do that by simply saying, "I need to think more about this. Can we come back to this in a day or two?" We can ask for more time with the full intention and commitment to engage in a process of discernment, not just push off the decision. Too many leaders push things off with no intention of coming back to them. Many do this hoping that time and space will cause people to forget, or they use it as a tactic to distract or divert attention and then force their way forward. Practicing discernment is hard work, but it is required of us if we want better outcomes for ourselves and our world.

PRACTICE PERSPECTIVE TAKING AND DISCERNMENT

Think about what areas of your life or leadership you feel strongly about—the areas that can create tension with others because you feel so strongly.

- What are these topics? Name them.

Consider the people in your life who see those areas in a different way than you do—ways that challenge the way you think, maybe even frustrate you.

- Who are these people? Name one or two for each area you wrote down.

Now if you really want to carry this out, solidify a next step you can take to have a conversation about these things.

- When will you see this person again?
- What questions would you like to ask to engage in a healthy dialogue that allows you to practice collaboration, perspective taking, and discernment?
- What might you need to do or not do in order to keep this conversation productive?

Practicing receiving support and employing these subsequent practices (collaboration, perspective taking, discernment) on our development journey and in our day-to-day life bring healing. They change the very nature of who we are by transforming what we believe and how we behave. That, in turn, changes our environment in a positive, sustainable way and allows us to bring ideas and innovation that can heal each other and the world. So get out there and invite someone in to improve your action plan, as you keep moving closer to the version of you that you're capable of being!

REFLECT ON YOUR JOURNEY

- What have you learned, unlearned, or relearned in this chapter?
- What has been most valuable to you?
- What one thing will you commit to doing differently going forward?
- Who can you invite in to keep you accountable?

CHAPTER 15

Integrating and Assessing

To this point we have built an action plan and had it refined by others. We have goals in place, and now we need a system to help us meet those goals. But this can be another place where we limit our ability to move forward successfully because we don't think through how we will execute, assess, and integrate our plan.

While we can't prepare for everything, and we don't want to get paralyzed in the planning process and prevent ourselves from taking action, we also want to be deliberate and intentional about how we move forward. That's where execution, assessment, and integration systems can help:

- Execution—You need to be able to see your progress, so you are more willing to stick to those goals.

- Assessment—You need a way to regroup when things aren't working, and have a plan for starting again, if needed.

- Integration—You need rewards for staying on track and consequences for not.

In developing your execution, assessment and integration systems, think about the process but don't overthink it. Give yourself a deadline to ensure you to do it and move on.

Let's return to Susan's action plan to use as our model:

Purpose Statement: I prioritize my needs and invest in my longevity, so I can maximize time with my family and my impact on the world.

New Truths:

1. I prioritize quality time with my family.

2. My health markers are in a good place.

3. My yeses will be used only for things that maximize my gifts, calling, and contributions.

Nonnegotiables:

1. Eat dinner with my family at least three nights per week.

2. Prioritize and plan family vacations.

3. Attend and be fully present at family events and activities.

Action Steps for New Truth 1 and Nonnegotiables:

- Perform review of my calendar and work habits (by [date]).

- Calendar daily white space time (8:00–10:00 a.m. and 4:00–5:00 p.m.).

- Calendar deep-work time (one hour per day).

- Identify person to triage email and build email triage plan and parameters.

- Implement email triage plan and checkpoints to review and adjust.

- Identify all tasks that can be handed off as well as people and plans for handoffs.

- Execute handoffs and schedule check-ins for any necessary adjustments.

- Audit personal commitments.

- Identify personal commitments to eliminate and build plan to adjust.

- Identify personal relationship priorities.

- Identify commitments needed to be made to spend time with those on the priority list.

STEPS FOR BUILDING YOUR EXECUTION, ASSESSMENT, AND INTEGRATION SYSTEM

First, to execute well, you want to make your action plan visible. Where can you put your action plan, so you see it every day? A bathroom mirror is an effective place because you are forced to see your plan alongside your face in the mirror. Visibility is the easiest and most impactful way you create accountability. You can put the whole thing up in one place, or you can write the purpose statement, New Truths, nonnegotiables, and current action step on sticky notes and place them where you feel called. The point is that you want what you are trying to accomplish to stay visible and top of mind.

Next is creating your execution system. When it comes to getting things done, everyone is wired differently. I have to take a multistep action and break it down into each step. Then, to ensure I actually do each step,

I transition the steps into my calendar. If it isn't in my calendar, it isn't happening! Let's walk through an example, and I'll share other ideas for how you can stay on track.

Looking back at Susan's action steps, let's work through the one named "Identify person to triage email and build email triage plan and parameters." We broke this down into more specific action steps:

1. Develop criteria for a person who would be effective in triaging email.

2. Populate a list of people who fit those criteria.

3. Select the top candidate.

4. Sketch a rough idea of what specifically you would be asking this person to do and how it would work.

5. Identify what has to be true for this person to be successful.

6. Make the ask of that person.

7. Schedule a time to create an email triage plan and parameters.

8. Select a date you will begin this new process.

9. Schedule a review within the first two weeks to discuss how it's going and to make improvements.

10. Create a process for further review and regrouping for continuous improvement and progress checks.

These steps may allow Susan to "complete" this action, depending on how she executes, integrates, and assesses them. Susan used her calendar, like I do, but you could use a checklist, OneNote, a visible work board, an Excel spreadsheet, or a project management tool. Just use a tool that will help you stay on task with each step and assign a timeline to it for completion, so you can keep it moving. Susan put all of these steps on her calendar based on a desired timeline of having the primary step fully executed within six weeks.

You need to follow this process for each of your action steps that require multiple steps so you can execute them. This system applies to strategic plan execution as an organization as well as carrying out a change within a team. If you aren't clear about each step—where you are with it and what's next—the day-to-day stuff can get in the way, and you won't make progress. This approach also helps ensure you have the capacity to follow through on what you are committing to.

Any change we make takes extra time and energy that many of us take for granted. Even when we block the time, we can overlook the mental and emotional load it takes on our energy. We can't do things as quickly when we are changing what we do. It's no wonder that in our personal and professional lives, we are regularly dropping the ball on things we have committed to. Breaking the action steps down helps us commit with a full understanding of what it will take to follow through on that commitment. We have to make space to think it through and outline what it will take.

Once you have all of your action steps broken down and outlined in an execution system, then it's time to develop an assessment system. When and how will you show and celebrate progress, and identify where you're stuck or off track and need to shift? In the midst of execution, it can be easy to overlook how and where things are changing and witness the progress we are making toward our goals. Small wins matter, and even if we aren't all the way to where we want to be, we want to show and celebrate the little shifts that will get us to the goals we've set. It's equally important to catch how we might be off track early so we can overcome any place where we are stuck or address anything that isn't working before it builds into something bigger or more challenging.

I suggest starting with five minutes at the end of each day, fifteen at the end of each week, and thirty at the end of each month to review where you met your commitments, where you fell short, and why. These reviews are meant to help you see your progress so you can celebrate it, and to show where you are stuck and struggling, so you can both celebrate and learn.

Again, this assessment system is so important because life gets busy, and we get distracted. Things will get in the way. If you set your calendar review time for 4:55 p.m. each weekday (4:45 p.m. on Fridays) and 4:30 p.m. on the last Friday of the month or something consistent like that, you will have the space and time (as well as reminders) to do the review. If you know you need extra support, also set up a system to review and check in with others: family members, friends, coaches, coworkers, etc., who are encouraging you in this journey. Investing this time to system-atize will help you stay on track, give you time to regroup, and add the accountability you need.

ESTABLISHING REWARDS AND CONSEQUENCES

Once you have your execution and assessment systems ready, the next task is setting up your integration system by building out rewards and consequences. What are the things you are committing to doing daily? Weekly? Monthly? How and when will you reward yourself for stick-ing to those? How and when will you implement consequences for not sticking to your commitments?

Aside from clarity and visibility, another reason we lack accountability is because there are no rewards or consequences for the change we are making. We have to think through and implement these because, let's face it, humans just aren't that naturally disciplined. We need the carrot and stick to keep us on track.

Susan had daily commitments for keeping white space on her calendar (at least one hour at the beginning and end of the day), doing one hour of deep-work time, and sticking to her diet and exercise plan. Susan loves to read, and she loves chocolate. She decided that if she stuck to her daily commitments, she could have a piece of dark chocolate after dinner, and if she stuck to her weekly commitments, she could spend thirty minutes in her favorite spot reading her book.

For some, the carrot alone will keep them on track. Others may need to think about what they will "take away" from themselves or what other consequences there will be if they don't follow through. This depends on your personality, and you know yourself best. I like to keep myself on track for the monthly things with more of the stick. For instance, if I don't follow through on a particular commitment, then I can't go on that trip, go to my favorite restaurant, etc.

Pick what works for you, but push yourself out of your comfort zone. If you naturally desire comfort, then you may need a consequence to push you to do what you've committed to. Or if something is harder or scarier, maybe you want a bigger reward or greater consequence for following through (or not) to keep you committed.

PLANNING YOUR (QUARTERLY) REVIEW

Plan a more in-depth review at least quarterly. In the early parts of a plan, I like to do a more in-depth review more often, so I can reassess the shift and what isn't working or what parts of the plan need to change. Again, there is no right way. Just find what works for you. During this more in-depth review, think about:

- What's going well and what's challenging?
- What feels good and what doesn't?
- What can't change and what needs to change?

Even when things are on track, I enjoy doing these reviews because it gives additional space for seeing progress and learning, and it also helps me grow in self-awareness and understanding. You'll start to pick up on nuances about yourself, your environment, your relationships, and other things that impact your plan. These microadjustments speed up progress and support more success. They also help things integrate into your life and schedule so you no longer have to think about them. You just do them.

MOVING INTO EXECUTION

Now you're ready to start executing the steps! You've got detailed steps with timelines, you have things visible and scheduled, you have multiple points of reflection and review, and you have a rewards and consequences system in place for yourself. This systematic approach allows you to put more of your time and energy into the actual execution because you have these buffers and bumpers in place to redirect you when you need it. That's called freedom within a framework . . . and it works!

Some of you reading this may think that all of this work of creating a system or thinking all of this through at this level isn't worth it. I assure you from my own experience and walking others through this process that this level of investment and discipline is what breeds the most success.

We want change and gratification right away. We don't like to do the hard work required to map this all out. While you need this discipline and rigidity out of the gate, you won't always need it as your self-awareness, discipline, and emotional intelligence grow.

Like anything, at the beginning, we need more parameters and infor-mation. When we are learning to swim, a good instructor doesn't throw us into the deep end of the pool or suggest we jump off the diving board. The instructor provides protective floating gear like a life jacket, and we take the stairs and wade into the water one step at a time. We get used to moving around in the water with the assistance of another.

At some point, when we are comfortable, we try to put our face in. We learn how to hold our breath before we can go all the way under or down the slide, and we need to learn a whole lot before we are ready to jump into and swim in the deep end. Eventually, we learn and get there. Eventually, we can show up at the pool and go straight to the diving board and jump in.

The same goes here. Allow yourself to get used to this way of discovering, exploring, learning, and growing, and eventually it will become second nature. All the steps you put in place to take something from intention to action will become natural. You will take pieces and parts of what's laid out here and apply them at the level you need to stay on track and continue to become your best self, intentionally.

ALLOWING A NEW WAY TO EMERGE

You are relearning a new way: a way to think, act, live, and lead more intentionally. You need to unlearn your old ways and learn this new process. Once you have time and repetition with the process, it will replace your old ways, and you won't have to try so hard. It will become integrated, a part of you—something you just do without thinking. You simply react. Now you want to move into intentional action. Be patient with yourself and keep pushing.

This new way takes more energy and more time. It is transforming you from the inside out. However many years of your life you've had until now, you've used them to build these patterns and habits, often without any awareness of them. It's going to take a good portion of time to unlearn all of that and to develop new ways. Celebrate progress. Little wins matter, and the recognition of them will keep you going.

This new way will help you remember how to listen to your heart. In the end, that's what this entire book is calling you back to. Quiet the noise and be intentional. Don't just float through life. Wake up to who you are and what you are called to. For those of you, like me, who have lived in your head most of your life, you will fight this. It will take you longer to come back to your heart and allow it to lead.

In forging a new way, a marker that we are on the right track is how uncomfortable we feel. The more uncomfortable, the more likely we are on the right track. Make a continuous, conscious effort to check in with your heart during this process. Our minds can lead us astray while our hearts are trying to take us to where we are meant to be. Putting my hand physically over my heart is always that little reminder for me to quiet the mind and allow my heart to speak. Let it be your guide as you reflect and reassess while you are executing these changes and new ways of seeing, doing, and being.

The world says that things should be easy, but we all know that greatness and anything worth doing takes energy and effort and will challenge us at the deepest level. Don't allow comfort to control you during this process. Don't accept your excuses. Do give yourself grace. By this I mean be disciplined and push yourself and at the same time be brutally honest about where you are and what you need. You will fail. That's OK. Learn the lesson and start again. You will need rest. Give yourself a breather and then dig back in.

Action is what heals. When we take steps forward, everything changes, and we change. Even if we don't reach what we set out to do, because we couldn't make it quite to the top of the mountain or because we decided after we learned something new that it was best to change course, any steps taken on the journey will change us.

Change isn't even the right word because it's something more substantial, deep, and profound that happens. We are transformed. By taking action, we are *restored*, not in the sense that we go back to how we were before, but in the sense that we become a better version of ourselves. Put everything you've got into taking action and fulfilling your commitments, and allow the path to continue to unfold itself along the way.

REFLECT ON YOUR JOURNEY

- What have you learned, unlearned, or relearned in this chapter?

- What has been most valuable to you?

- What one thing will you commit to doing differently going forward?

- Who can you invite in to keep you accountable?

CHAPTER 16

Sharing What You've Learned

As you take action and give yourself space for review and reflection, learning and lessons will surface. New ways of thinking will emerge. As you feel comfortable and called, share with others what you are learning and what is changing. To this point we have been focused on what we can do to live and lead more intentionally, and to experience more peace, confidence, and freedom on the journey to reach our potential.

But this isn't about us. Or maybe it's *about* us but it's not *for* us. We were born to know and love and serve. We are doing all of this work to be free of the negative thoughts, patterns, and habits that hold us back from becoming our best self so that we can contribute to the world in the highest possible way. We are doing all of this work so we can be free of ourselves in order to serve others.

Share early, share often, share always. There is no perfect time to share; it's just important that we share. Each of us is at a different point in our journey, and there is so much power in perspective and story. Yours can certainly help someone else, and there will always be someone who has a perspective and story that could help you. But we only know this if we share them with one another.

> ## THINGS TO CONSIDER SHARING
>
> Here are a few big questions to get you thinking about what you could share:
> - What are you learning?
> - How have you changed?
> - What have been the toughest challenges you've faced on this journey?
> - What is better today and why?

THE IMPACT OF SHARING YOUR EXPERIENCE

"I know that place" is a phrase that I have come to love with all my heart. It makes me feel seen, heard, and known. In my own journey, there have been (and will be) times I desperately need to hear those words. I can't hear or hold them close if I'm not willing to open up and share my journey with others.

One of my coaches uttered these words to me during one of the darkest and lowest points of my life. I had left the comfort and safety of a successful corporate career to pursue this dream that God placed on my heart, but I was in the messy middle. It felt as if I had lost all sense of who I was, my whole identity. I had left something good behind with no idea of where I was going.

I shared that I felt like "an untethered balloon floating around in complete darkness with no idea if or where I might find the ground again" (as you might recall me mentioning in Chapter 6). Those words came from somewhere deep inside me. As I spoke them out loud, they surprised me and although they made sense in my heart and they felt completely right, in my head the words sounded strange, even ludicrous.

Just at the moment I started to explain myself, my coach interrupted me with those sweet, piercing words: "I know that place." At that moment, I fell apart, not because I was frustrated, frightened, or sad, but because I was so relieved. This man sitting in front of me was someone I admired and respected with my whole being, and he had felt this way too? Hallelujah!

I cried and laughed through the tears explaining how grateful I was that I was not alone. He shared that more than one time in his life, he had been in "that place." He shared all of himself with me—what happened, how he felt, what he learned, how he was transformed, what happened next—all of it. I drank in those stories as if I were right there beside him.

While he was sharing, there were so many things I could relate to in his words. They were completely different circumstances, but I could draw the parallels and see how his story and lessons might apply to my own. When he was done sharing, his simple encouragement was to stay in that place and do the work to find my way out. He reassured me that this space was temporary and the fear and pain I was experiencing were all part of the lessons and transformation that were mine to have.

"Just don't quit and don't try to avoid these feelings," he said. He knew my pattern. I wanted to feel safe and secure. I could allow myself to be talked into going back to my "OK" existence. I would rather do just about anything than feel completely vulnerable like that untethered balloon floating around in the dark without a foundation. But his story inspired me to stay in it. If how I felt was the price to become more like him, I could do it. He was one of the kindest, most generous, and most peaceful persons I had ever had the pleasure of knowing.

Although we are all on different paths and different places along the path, the journey that we humans take is more similar than it is different. Someone has experienced what you are going through before, and someone will experience what you are going through now. Just as you learned from others' experiences, others will have the chance to learn from yours. That is the power of sharing your experience.

WHY WE HESITATE TO SHARE OUR EXPERIENCE

Many things can hold us back from sharing. The obvious is shame and guilt that we are not perfect. We don't share what we are going through because many of us believe that we should have known or done better, and if we had, we wouldn't be in this place. This way of thinking is not kind or helpful to you or anyone around you. We stifle a lot of learning and growing that could take place in ourselves and in the world around us because of our shame and guilt.

Another reason we don't share is that we like to think we don't need any help. We enjoy believing we have things figured out, or even that we are better than someone else. That is the safer play from an emotional and vulnerability standpoint, but it is not the way to reach your potential and is not what good leaders choose. The best in our world consistently choose humility and vulnerability, and by doing so, they change the world.

In the first two years of The Restoration Project's existence, my teammates and I had a lot of feedback from older white men telling us that the name of our organization was too soft and that people would be "put off" by the idea that they or their organization needs restoration. Eventually, when I built enough courage, I simply responded, "Anyone who feels this way is exactly the type of leader who needs our work the most."

The truth is that all of us are and always will be on a never-ending journey to improve if we want to reach our full potential. No one "makes it" in a way in which they are perfect and doing everything right. Those who think that way or have settled into "this is just the way I am" have a closed, fixed mindset.

Many people are too afraid to admit where they are. They don't have the courage and discipline to face the truth to continue their growth. Their insecurity and fear just won't let them. These people show up in the world threatening, intimidating, and manipulating others in an attempt to maintain power and control. They will tell you that this work and most of the concepts in it are "soft" or "irrelevant."

Let them. Stay committed to your life and your journey. Keep elevating your life, your leadership, your energy. It may be lonely because the sad truth is that many will not attempt this journey. They do not believe they can change, or they simply aren't interested. This brings me to another reason we become scared to share our story with others.

LETTING GO TO GROW

You will have to leave people behind. There will be people in your life who don't want you to fulfill your potential because that means you will no longer engage in toxic relationships and life patterns that have been created. As you elevate, they will do anything they can to pull you back down. You have a hard choice to make: Will you allow them to keep you where you are, or will you let them go so you can grow?

This has been a common occurrence and narrative in my story. When I started my healing journey, I was firmly planted in unhealthy patterns and relationships with people that were long and deep. Most of them I had created myself out of my own wounds. Because I had felt unsafe for most of my life, I had become very good at controlling people and situations so that I could maintain my own sense of security.

When people close to me had an issue, they called me and I got involved. I rescued, protected, and enabled . . . and they let me. I became their security blanket. Anytime there was an issue, call Lindsay, she'll know what to do or she'll even fix it for me! As I became aware of this pattern, I realized how much resentment I had toward some of the people I was rescuing, protecting, and enabling. I started to see how I was allowing everyone else's problems to distract me from my own.

I started developing new patterns. When someone called with a problem, instead of fixing it or engaging with it, I gave them their power back by handing the issue back to them. I asked, "What are you going to do about this?" Or in a milder example, I simply asked, "Is there anything you need from me in this situation?" See, sometimes the person didn't really want me to do anything; they just wanted me to listen.

But those who relied on me to fix things for them got upset. They didn't like this new responsibility to take care of things themselves. They blamed me for their issues, called me names, tried to make me feel like a bad person for not getting involved, and on and on. I needed the support of friends, family, healers, coaches, and counselors around me to process it all and stay on track.

Sharing with others won't always be easy. For those who want what's best for you, you will get support and encouragement and maybe even hear, "I know that place." From those who want to stay stagnant in their lives, who are unwilling to change and therefore believe no one else should change, from them there will be challenges. You will have to work hard to find new people, your people, as you evolve.

SHARING IN THE MIDST OF OUR IMPERFECTIONS

Another big reason we don't share is because we think, "Who are we to help someone else?" Our self-doubt blocks us from deep connection with others more times than we can count. This is especially true among humble leaders. We know that we don't know everything. We know that we aren't perfect. These truths hold us back from sharing what we do know.

When I went out on my own to launch The Restoration Project, I was very resistant to the title of coach for this very reason. I didn't have it all figured out, so how could I help anyone else? Then my coach asked me, "When will you know enough or be healed enough to believe you are ready to help someone else?" I sat with that question for a long time, stupefied, because the answer was *never.* I felt defeated at first, but that was exactly his point. Start where you are and help who you can based on your experience.

This journey of learning and growing and healing and developing will never end. None of us will ever reach our potential in this life. We can only die trying. Along the way, each of us will have different experiences and learn different lessons, and the more we share those, the more we can learn and grow and develop as a whole.

This brings me to the last reason we don't share: We don't know how or where to start. I hope that I have overcome all the objections you have in your mind and in your heart and that now you are fully ready to share. But how? I won't get into the specifics of how you bring your story up to someone or into a conversation, because you are smart enough to figure that out, but I do want to give you a few tips on how to share your story so that you feel comfortable and confident doing it.

SHARING YOUR STORY

First, check your heart and your spirit. You want to be sure that you are sharing your story and perspective in an open-hearted and open-minded way that allows the other person to have a different perspective or opinion about what you say. You can share what is happening to you and how it makes you feel and what lessons you are learning. You are offering these things up as *your* truth, not *the* truth.

Sometimes, people can share their story and perspective in a way that leads to them telling us what we need to do or that we need to do what they did. Please do not use sharing your story as an opportunity to try and teach a lesson or tell someone what to do. Your goal is not to convince anyone of anything or to get them to do anything; it's simply to provide that point of connection and your perspective as an offering. It's the other person's choice what they do with it.

Keep the energy of your story with you. When we share something difficult or heavy, we can find ourselves desiring the other person to console us, commiserate with us, or even fix the issue. This is draining for the other person. I know you have felt this before in your own interactions. Share your story with the resolve that you are responsible for what happens next and you are not expecting anything from them. Don't put that energy on someone else.

Consider what is appropriate to share. There is a line between professional and personal, personal and private. You have to decide who is ready for an invitation into your private life. Protect yourself and others by keeping private matters or that level of depth in the story between you and the people you trust and care about the most.

It's also important to remember that as you become more open to others and willing to be vulnerable, they may not want to engage in that level of intimacy with you. That might make them feel uncomfortable. Ask if you aren't sure. This might also be circumstantial. You might share a story one way in one-on-one conversation with a friend and a completely different way with a group at work. Be mindful and intentional about what and how you share.

Finally, release any expectations you have around sharing. It's only when we freely give our story to the world that it has the most impact. We don't share to gain attention or affection, accolades or affirmation.

We know our intentions are pure and we are sharing rightly when we are sharing simply to support and serve another.

Remember, becoming your best self might be *about* you but it's not *for* you. Get out and share the hope, peace, and love you are experiencing and the wisdom you are gaining with the world!

In Reflection

As I sit here working on the last part of this book, I find myself challenged to complete it. First, because I am fearful of sharing my voice and my heart with the world. Second, because I know that the minute this gets published in black and white, I will know more than I did at the initial writing and wish to change it.

But these are exactly two of the many reasons for getting this book into the world. I want you to find your voice and share it with others, no matter how scary that is. This morning, I had a client text me the following message, "Just a quick update . . . I have been practicing my assertiveness at work, and I am finding that some people really don't like it. Thank you so much for helping me find my voice."

Interesting that in this message, she conveys that she is being met with resistance, and yet she is grateful for the encouragement to do it anyway. This is what living from our integrity and our heart looks and feels like. Regardless of the actions or reactions of others, we can confidently keep sharing and speaking up because we aspire for positive change in the world. That will bring resisters and naysayers. We will do it anyway.

Living an intentional life you won't regret takes courage—courage to heal your heart and soul so you can genuinely act from a place of wholeness with no resentment and no regrets. It takes work—work to evaluate and reevaluate our thoughts, feelings, and actions so we can show up at our best. Discipline to keep growing.

We can only get there through surrender and simplicity. Surrendering our ego. Opening our hands and our hearts to what is versus what we wish could be. Letting go of all that we want for all that we have. Releasing who we were, so we can become who we were meant to be. Quieting the noise of culture and our own desires, so we can come back to what truly matters. Clearing out the negativity, the striving, and all the vices we use to temporarily fill us up, so we can reach the truest parts of ourselves and find out what it can feel like to truly find contentment.

As I sit here, I know that the frameworks, concepts, and resources in this book will be things I keep coming back to for the remainder of my life. Just when I feel like I have it figured out, something will happen, and I will have to start the journey again. I feel unsettled and settled about that fact all at the same time.

I know that I will die attempting to really know myself and to reach my potential. So instead of using all of my energy to do that, I will balance my own inner work with a focus on the people and the world around me and the good works and service I can provide them. In doing that work, I will also be refined and make new discoveries and connections that bring me back to myself all over again. I will continue to become a more restored human and leader shown by these characteristics:

aware	confident	honest
present	compassionate	connected
curious	courageous	calm
clear	open	committed

kind	disciplined	composed
patient	steady	undisturbed
gentle	poised	friendly
positive	dignified	gracious
generous	honorable	merciful
considerate	cheerful	true
stable	lighthearted	understanding
grounded	expansive	brave

I hope you will use this book and the concepts in it to reconnect with yourself, with others, and with the world to become a more restored version of you. I hope you continue to go after your own heart and pursue what is true to you, the deepest and purest parts of you, in any given moment. You are changing, and so your needs and desires will change. Use your heart as a guide. The world needs you.

DO YOUR WORK TO THEN BE HEALED

In closing, I must share that my hope for this book is that it helps you do your work. By that, I mean increasing your self-awareness and getting to know yourself and your gifts to improve your confidence and encourage you to use your voice. This is a critical part in all of our journeys as human beings.

But doing this work and being healed are two separate things. The first brings awareness and understanding that changes who we are in a positive way. The second invites us into a deeper level of transformation that allows healing within ourselves, others, and the world.

To get to that level requires something else entirely. It's something we cannot give ourselves; we can only receive it. To be healed we must receive the love, grace and mercy that only Jesus can provide. That is for another conversation and maybe another book altogether. Regardless of what you believe, I want you to know that you are loved more than you could ever imagine and more than any human being is capable of understanding.

God is pursuing you. No matter what you have done or where you have been, He is still in pursuit. He wants your heart. He wants you. All of you. I know it, and I hope someday you are able to experience and receive all the love that is available to you, because you are lovely, you are loved.

Allow yourself to fully see you. Allow God to fully see you. As you're ready, allow others to see you too and then be free. We need more healed leaders. We cannot pursue the healing and positive transformation of our families, communities, workplaces, and the world until we are fully committed to our own work and healing. Do your work, then be healed. We need you.

Index of Exercises, Frameworks, and Questions

EXPLORATION EXERCISES

REFLECTION QUESTIONS

Chapter 1

- What does a good life look like for me?
- What will matter in the end?
- What would I do if money didn't matter?
- Where in my life have I not kept my promises?
- Where am I out of my integrity?
- Where am I not telling the full truth?
- Who am I beneath all the labels?
- What is meaningful and valuable to me?
- What values do I hold close?

Chapter 2

- What experiences have shaped my life?
- How did these experiences make me feel? What was I believing as they happened?
- What are some common emotions and behaviors that show up in my life?
- What could this emotion mean? Where might these emotions have originated?
- What beliefs do I hold true about myself?
- Where could these beliefs have originated? What patterns and habits have these created in my life?
- What beliefs do I hold true about others and the world?
- Where could these beliefs have originated? What patterns and habits have these created in my life?

Chapter 3

- What are the small moments in my life in which I can start to create awareness of my thoughts and feelings?
- How am I feeling in this moment? What am I thinking about right now? What thoughts, words, or phrases are on my mind?
- Which thoughts do I need to let go of or shift? What is one thing I can do to improve the stories I am telling myself?
- Who are the people that speak into my life the most?
- Who do I trust, admire, and respect? (name at least five people)
  - How are they impacting my life?

- What influence do they have on my thoughts and actions?

- If I wished they were more influential in my life, what might that look like and how could we make that happen?

Chapter 4

- What thought patterns keep showing up in my life?

  - Where did these originate or what are they rooted in?

  - What do these thoughts say about me?

  - How do these thought patterns impact my view of myself, others, and the world?

- What behavioral patterns keep showing up in my life?

  - Where did these originate or what are they rooted in?

  - What do these behaviors say about me?

  - How do these behavioral patterns impact my view of myself, others, and the world?

- What patterns in my habits keep showing up in my life?

  - Where did these originate or what are they rooted in?

  - What do these habits say about me?

  - How do these habit patterns impact my view of myself, others, and the world?

- What's the first thing I do when I wake up in the morning?

How does this make me feel? How does this impact my thoughts and mood for the day?

- What other routines do I notice about my morning?

- What would my ideal morning look and feel like?

- What are the most important and impactful elements in that ideal morning?

- If I could only include one element from that morning routine, what would it be?

- How can I incorporate that into my routine starting tomorrow?

- What does my typical evening look like?

- How do I feel in the evenings?

- What's the last thing I do before I go to bed?

- How might all of this be impacting my relationships? My goals? My overall sense of peace? My sleep?

- What would my ideal evening routine look and feel like?

- What are the most important and impactful elements in that ideal evening?

- If I could include one element from that evening routine, what would it be?

- How can I incorporate that into my routine starting tomorrow?

- What words would I use to describe the leaders I admire most? What do people who can live out those words do?

- What kind of habits and routines do the leaders I admire most have in their life and work?

- What are the thoughts and beliefs of the leaders I admire most?

- What false narratives or limiting beliefs have been built out of my patterns? What do these patterns say to the world about who I am?

- What impacts have my patterns had on me? On my relationships? On my work? In my leadership?

- What pattern is my first priority to change in a positive way?

Chapter 5

- How does feedback make me feel?

- Does it validate something I know or desire to be true about me? Does it conflict with my self-image? Which parts are easy to accept? Which parts are difficult to accept?

- How did the feedback I received shift my perception about myself, others, and my worldview?

Chapter 6

- What does this limiting belief mean?

- What is my new starting place?

- What skills or practices do I need to develop to live this out?

- Are there areas of life where I feel out of alignment or out of my integrity?

- What support do I need to stay on track through this part of my restoration process?

- Who could I reach out to and invite in to support me?

- What positive affirmations or routines could I put in place that will prevent me from giving up or reverting back to old ways?

Chapter 8

- What matters most right now?
- What is valuable to me?
- List the five people you spend the most time with.
- List the five people you admire most and who you'd like to spend more time with.
- List some ways you could be in contact with each person you listed and get more time with them.
- List the top five things that take up your time right now.
- List the top five things that take up your energy right now.
- List the top five things you spend your money on right now.
- What does this picture tell me?
- How do these answers match up, or not, with what's meaningful and valuable to me? Or in other words, where am I aligned and where do I need to make adjustments?
- What is one thing I can do to get more aligned?
- What will it look and feel like to be fully aligned in this area?
- What would be different if I was aligned in this area?
- What impacts would it have on me and those around me?
- What do I have control over? What don't I have control over?
- What trade-offs or decisions do these realities force me to face?
- What do I need to start or stop doing?
- What are the milestones: outcomes I will see or changes I will make? By when?
- Who can I lean on for support?

- What happens if I backslide?
- List the five people you spend the most time with at work.
- List the five people you admire most in your professional life that you'd like to spend more time with.

Chapter 9

- What do I desire?
- What drives me?
- What makes me feel alive?
- What causes do I care about?
- What other passions come to mind for me?
- What am I known for?
- What do people regularly compliment me for?
- What are my strengths?
- What comes naturally to me?
- What gives me energy?
- What are the deep longings I've consistently ignored?
- If I could do anything, what would I do?
- If I could be anyone, who would I be?
- Who am I at my best? (What am I doing? How am I feeling?)
- How would I like people to describe me when I'm not around or remember me when I'm gone?
- What does success mean to me?
- What will matter most in the end?

Chapter 10

- What do you see that I don't?
- What are my unique gifts?
- Why is this vision possible? What could get in the way?

Chapter 11

- Why do I want these new things?
- What impact could these new things have (on me, on my relationships, in my life, on my career, etc.)?
- What do I want to create in the world?

Chapter 12

- What needs to change for me to live more fully aligned?
- What heart shifts need to take place?
- What mindset shifts need to happen?
- What behaviors need to start, stop, and continue?
- What habits and routines need to start, stop, and continue?
- What practices need to start, stop, and continue?

Chapter 13

- What will be different?
- How will I know I've arrived or am successful?
- What cannot change?
- What must be in place for my New Truths to become true?

- What are the gaps between where I am and where want to be?
- What are the steps to make those shifts?

Chapter 14

- What are the areas of my life or leadership I feel strongly about (areas that can create tension with others because I feel so strongly)?
- Who are the people in my life who see those areas in a different way than I do?
    - When will I see this person again?
    - What questions would I like to ask to engage in a healthy dialogue that allows me to practice collaboration, perspective taking, and discernment?
    - What might I need to do or not do to keep this conversation productive?

Chapter 15

- What's going well and what's challenging?
- What feels good and what doesn't?
- What can't change and what needs to change?

Chapter 16

- What am I learning?
- How have I changed?
- What have been the toughest challenges I've faced on this journey?
- What is better today and why?

Index

Acknowledgments

I have loved and lost so many people, as I'm sure you have. Loving and losing big has reminded me that my life matters a whole lot, and at the same time, not much at all. This perspective has given me new hope and freedom. It has me consistently asking myself: What will I do with my life? Who will I become?

Thank you to all of the people who love me big in all of the beautiful, brutal, and boring moments of life. To those who have allowed me into their lives in deep and meaningful ways, and wanted to be part of mine, thank you for allowing me to be me—always learning, growing, and changing. Thank you for loving me because of me and in spite of me.

Thank you to God for giving me the purpose, passion, and willpower to put this book on paper. Thank you for all the gifts and blessings you have given me in this life and for making this book even possible.

Thank you to my husband for being my number one challenger and cheerleader in every aspect of life. Thank you for being my safe place and loving me, especially when I couldn't love myself. I would not be who I am today without you. You make me better.

Thank you to my best friends and teammates, Brooke and Sarah, for encouraging me to shine my light bright and use my unique gifts for good. Thank you for believing in this dream and leaning in to make it ours . . . something so much better than I ever dreamed it could be.

Thank you to my mom and sister for your never-ending love and support, and for allowing me to push the boundaries and learn on my own, even when it was difficult for you to witness. Thank you for encouraging me and challenging me all along the way. You have shaped me and blessed me. Especially you, Momma.

Thank you to my Grandma Dick up in heaven smiling down. Thank you for being my angel in pink through all my hard days.

Thank you to Geery, Jai, Toni, and Karly for your special support in allowing this book to be realized through me.

Thank you to the clients of The Restoration Project for believing in us and allowing us to serve you. It is truly an honor and privilege to support you on your journey!

Thank you to the rest of my friends and family for your love and for picking up this book to support me and helping this dream of writing a book to come true!

Thank you to you, the reader. I celebrate your desire to create positive, systemic transformation within yourself and within the world and for possessing a burning desire to live life to the fullest and leave an impact. Thank you for reading and for doing your work. We need you. The world needs you. To dream again. To reawaken to the hope and possibilities. To rise above the challenges, troubles, and divides. To capitalize on the truth, beauty, and goodness inside you and all around you. You are the hope for our future.

About the Author

Author photo by studioU. www.studiouphotography.com

Lindsay is a proud wife, daughter, auntie, and friend. She is passionate about Jesus, hugs, dreams, adventures, and writing. She is the author of the blog *Grit, Gratitude, and Grace* and founder of The Restoration Project. Lindsay's personal adversity story, coupled with her leadership and business strategy experience, is the foundation of her reflective, inspirational, and disciplined coaching style.

When she isn't pursuing the things mentioned above, Lindsay enjoys volunteering, making memories with friends and family, spending time with her husband, and being outdoors. She and her husband love the Midwest and reside in Iowa, where she attempts to share love and hope with everyone she meets.

ABOUT THE RESTORATION PROJECT

The Restoration Project is a women-owned coaching and consulting practice based in Iowa. We specialize in experiences, programs, and services that challenge individuals and organizations to explore identity and intentions for the sake of improving leadership and organizational effectiveness, as well as individual well-being. These experiences provide space for clients to become more aware and intentional, so they can positively transform the way they live, lead, and work.

Our process is reflective, emergent, and created with our clients, which allows us to go deeper and create sustainable change. We work with individuals and organizations across the world who have big dreams for positive change and systemic transformation, and are willing to put in the work to see it through. Clients who work with us experience restored hearts and minds, clarity and calm in chaos, confidence where there is uncertainty and doubt, and an increase in collective connection, commitment, and success.

Our Vision: A world filled with individuals and organizations who live, lead, and work with meaning on their journey to reach their full potential.

Our Mission: Build Connection, Restore Intention, and Inspire Action.

Our **Values:** Understand Yourself and Honor Others. Live with Courage. Lead with Love. Act with Integrity. Connect to Something Greater.

You can reach us at the-restorationproject.com or email us at info@the-restorationproject.com

Printed in the USA
CPSIA information can be obtained
at www.ICGtesting.com
LVHW050402041024
792855LV00005B/147

9 781632 998705